– LLEWELLYN'S –

2022

HERBAL

ALMANAC

© 2021 Llewellyn Publications
Llewellyn Publications is a registered trademark of
Llewellyn Worldwide Ltd.

Cover Designer: Kevin R. Brown
Editor: Lauryn Heineman

Interior Art: © Melani Huggins
Garden plan illustrations on pages 270–71
by Llewellyn Art Department

You can order annuals and books from *New Worlds,*
Llewellyn's catalog. To request a free copy, call 1-877-
NEW WRLD toll-free or visit www.llewellyn.com.

ISBN: 978-0-7387-6044-5
Llewellyn Worldwide Ltd.
2143 Wooddale Drive
Woodbury, MN 55125-2989

Printed in the United States of America

Contents

DIY and Crafts

Plant Profiles

Gardening Resources

Introduction to
Llewellyn's Herbal Almanac

Gardening and self-sufficiency have skyrocketed in popularity since the start of the global pandemic. Confinement to the home inspired a boom in growing plants both indoors and out. While adapting to the new normal, many people sought more sustainable lifestyles, causing at various times shortages of yeast and canning supplies as many people—some for the first time—embarked upon bread-baking journeys and preserved homegrown food for their family to enjoy in the winter months.

There is no better time to grow, use, and eat herbs than now, and we hope you'll find inspiration for your own healthy life in this book. With sage advice appealing to novice gardeners and experienced herbalists alike, our experts tap into the practical and historical aspects of herbal knowledge—using herbs to help you connect with the earth, enhance your culinary creations, and heal your body and mind.

In addition to the twenty-three articles written by Master Gardeners, professors, and homesteaders, this book offers reference materials tailored specifically for successful growing and gathering. Use this book to log important dates, draw your garden plan, practice companion planting, garden by the moon, find a helpful herbal remedy, and keep track of goals and chores in the personal logbook pages.

Reclaiming our connection to Mother Earth in our own backyards can bring us harmony and balance—and a delicious, healthy harvest. May your garden grow tall and your dishes taste divine!

Growing
and
Gathering

Alpine Rock Gardens

⤜ Elizabeth Barrette ⤛

Rock gardening offers an interesting variation from more common types of gardening. It is especially well suited to growing herbs because the gritty soil and stone mulch discourage weeds, and the low amount of nutrients concentrates flavors in the leaves. Since many herbs come from rocky or mountainous habitats, they thrive in rock gardens. You can choose from plants that grow on lower slopes or the true alpines that cling to mountaintops. They're all beautiful, and many are also useful.

What Is an Alpine Rock Garden?

An alpine garden features plants from a mountainous environment. Such places tend to be harsh. They are more often cold than warm and more often dry than wet. The soil tends to be thin, sandy or rocky, and poor. Specifically, *alpine* means above the tree level, so these are low-growing plants. You can also choose plants that grow in scree or on cliffs farther down. While not all alpine gardens are also rock gardens, many of them are, due to the nature of mountainous soil.

A rock garden features stones large and small. It provides a home for plants that love rocky, well-drained, often poor soil. In some cases, there's very little soil at all, with plants growing on or between the stones. The plants may come from one area or many, but they need to enjoy similar conditions. So a rock garden may emulate a hot desert, a chilly mountaintop, or even a sheer cliff. Often a number of boulders form the focus, surrounded by sand or gravel. A rock garden may also be alpine, but it doesn't have to be.

Rock gardens are very flexible in size, so you can suit them to your budget and available space. You can make anything from a miniature container garden to a wall spanning the length of your yard.

An alpine rock garden, then, is a combination of these two types. It re-creates the conditions, as closely as possible, of a stony mountain meadow or outcropping. The gritty soil makes it drain well, and it needs very little water because plants adapted to such conditions are quite frugal with water.

Sometimes all the plants come from the same mountainous region, which makes it easier for them to get along. Other times they come from different regions, which adds diversity. The stones, however, should look like they go together so that the rock garden achieves a natural and harmonious appearance. It may even become a haven for local wildlife that loves a rocky environment.

Suitable Rocks and Other Hardscaping

Unlike most gardens, a rock garden is primarily defined by its hardscaping. It has a container or a frame to support it. Inside, the soil is sandy or rocky. Larger stones or boulders provide a visual focus. All this rock mass creates a heat sink. If you live in a chilly climate, that's good, so choose darker rocks to enhance the effect. If you live in a hot, sunny climate, you don't want to cook your plants, so consider lighter rocks.

Fine gravel can be used to cover soil or mix into it, as well as to line paths. Decomposed granite is the smallest and most nourishing for plants. It's not too rich and makes a nice home for alpine plants. Crushed granite has crisp edges, which discourage pests, while pea gravel is rounded, a more restful appearance.

Pebbles are generally used to cover the soil surface. River rock is smooth, often multicolored, and looks very nice. Lava rock is quite sharp, ideal if you want to deter slugs and snails, but it has a harsher look.

Flagstones are flat pavers. Include a dark one as a basking stone to attract beneficial insects and cold-blooded wildlife. Slate is most often silver to gray. It's soft, so choose this if you want your garden to weather and look old. Sandstone mostly comes in warm colors and has a rough texture. It is very durable. Basalt is dark gray to black, perfect for absorbing heat. It also has the unusual quality of absorbing sound well, making it ideal for noisy locations.

Boulders are bigger rocks that may be rough or rounded. Granite is a very hard stone that comes in all colors. It is among the most durable. Limestone is usually light to medium in color. It weathers quickly in acidic conditions, which can be good or bad depending on your opinion of entropy in the garden.

Sometimes boulders are sold not based on stone type but on covering, typically moss or lichen. Usually lichen suits an alpine garden better, but if you are replicating a damp mountain (like those mostly covered in fog), then moss can work too. However, these are expensive. With a little patience, you can use a recipe of soil, yogurt, and ground plants to encourage lichens or moss to sprout on a bare rock.

Others are sold by shape. Block boulders are squarish and can be used to build walls, especially the kind where you can plant things in the cracks. Bench boulders are even bigger. Both of these make excellent edging for rock gardens.

Most planters are ceramic, an ideal home for small rock gardens. You can even keep these in the house if you choose plants suited to those conditions. Concrete troughs are also popular, although they tend to weather quickly.

There is one unique material prized for alpine rock gardens, and that is tufa. This porous rock forms when lime-rich water evaporates. Therefore, alpine plants can grow right into the stone itself. It is available in large hollowed pieces for use as a container and smaller solid pieces as accents. Tufa gravel is smaller and will not compact. Tufa soil is decayed stone and very nourishing for alpine plants. These are not cheap but can greatly increase your chances of success.

Some people like to add statues or other ornaments to their rock gardens. Among the more popular ones are ceramic or concrete figures. Bear in mind that concrete will weather fast, while glazed ceramic is more resistant. Bronze is spectacular but very expensive. Chinese lanterns of concrete, ceramic, or metal make a lovely addition to an Asian-themed garden. Glass can be an interesting choice, as chunks of slag resemble colorful rocks. You can also get gazing balls in any color, some that even glow in the dark. Avoid birdfeeders or birdbaths as the droppings from visitors will enrich the soil too much.

Appropriate Herbs and Other Plants

Alpine plants grow at high altitudes in harsh conditions. They include woody and herbaceous plants, deciduous and evergreen. Some grow from bulbs, corms, or tubers. However, few alpines are annuals. They tend to be small and tough, often creeping or cushioning in form. Therefore, they suffer little damage from wind or snow. Small leaves, often hairy or leathery, minimize water loss, according to Let's Go Gardening. Their sturdy roots dig into the rocky soil in search of scarce nutrients and water, even growing into cracks between the stones. If you want to xeriscape a garden to reduce watering, this is a great way. An advantage in herbs is that poor, dry soil tends to concentrate the active components, making for potent, flavorful herbs. Avoid fertilizing too much as this can cause abundant foliage with little flavor.

Allium is the onion genus. It has many members, all highly resistant to pests due to the pungent flavor. Alpine leek (*Allium victorialis*) has broad, strappy leaves sprouting from a root-stalk. It grows in the Caucasus and Himalayas. Alpine rosy bells (*A.*

oreophilum) are more ornamental with bright pink blossoms. Pacific mountain onion (*A. validum*) has narrower leaves with a pink pom-pom of flowers. The bulb, leaves, and flowers are all edible. This wild onion is common across the Cascade Range, the Sierra Nevada, and the Rocky Mountains. Blue Mountain onion (also known as Cuddy Mountain onion, *A. fibrillum*) has very thin leaves and white flowers. It spans eastern Washington and Oregon to Idaho and Montana. Mountain chive (*A. monanthum*) has little round bulbs and long tubular leaves. It comes from Korea, Japan, and China.

Aster is another huge family, of which some members live at altitude. Alpine aster (*Aster alpinus*) has daisylike flowers of white, pink, purple, or blue. It is native to the Alps. Western mountain aster (*Symphyotrichum spathulatum*) is similar in appearance. It grows throughout the western United States with highest density in the Sierra Nevada.

Bearberry (*Arctostaphylos uva-ursi*) is a very low-growing plant with leathery leaves found throughout the subarctic area of the Northern Hemisphere. It bears beautiful urn-shaped flowers followed by berries that are edible but not very tasty. The leaves are dried for smoking.

Beardtongue has many species spanning a variety of habitats. Cliff beardtongue (*Penstemon rupicola*) is a mat-forming subshrub from the west coast of North America, including the Klamath Mountains. It has rounded leaves and flowers that range from pink to purple. Consider this a candidate for wall gardens as it clings well to vertical surfaces.

Bellflower is a popular rock garden plant. Rough bellflowers (*Campanula scabrella*) form a small clump that sends up blue to purple flowers. It is native to the western United

States, often growing in the scree at the base of mountains. It's a great choice if you want a gravel garden.

Crocus is a quintessential flower of spring that comes in white, purple, yellow, and combinations. It has a wide range and thrives in the well-drained, sandy soil of alpine rock gardens. Some, like *Crocus tommasinianus*, seed so enthusiastically that they are ideal for naturalizing, but they can become weeds in a rock garden. Choose thoughtfully.

Cyclamen puts out autumn leaves that yield to winter flowers in shades from white through pink to magenta. *Cyclamen coum* comes from the mountains around the Black Sea and from Turkey. *C. alpinum* is a related species.

Daisy spans many habitats. Alpine or cutleaf daisy (*Erigeron compositus*) has a compact cushion of wooly, gray-green leaves. It produces cheerful flowers in white to pink with a yellow center. It lives across much of Canada and Alaska, along with high altitudes in the western United States.

Dianthus is a popular garden flower, but some wild types are hardier. Alpine pink (*Dianthus alpinus*) is a mat-forming plant that puts out pink flowers with white spots. The cultivated versions come in colors from white to pink and purple to red.

Dwarf iris (*Iris reticulata*) is a miniature version of larger iris flowers. Swordlike leaves sprout from small bulbs. Various colors include deep blue, periwinkle, and yellow. It hails from the cold dry mountains of Turkey, Iraq, Iran, and Russia.

Edelweiss (*Leontopodium nivale*) is a mountain wildflower with white blossoms. It likes rocky limestone environments in the Alps and the Carpathians. In traditional medicine, it offers a remedy for abdominal and respiratory complaints.

Fir includes a wide variety of trees and shrubs. Smaller examples do well in rock gardens. However, they need more water than usual for alpine plants. Dwarf balsam fir (*Abies balsamea*) is popular for its dense mounding habit and sweet resinous fragrance. Balsam firs have been used to make incense. They are native to much of North America.

Glory-of-the-snow (*Scilla* sect. *Chionodoxa*) is an alpine flower that blooms just as the snow begins to melt. Its flowers may be white, pink, or blue. It comes from Crete, Cyprus, and Turkey.

Juniper is a genus that spans a vast range across several continents. Alpine juniper (*Juniperus communis*) can be a small tree or a very low sprawling shrub, easily sculpted by wind or pruning shears. This species delivers most of the juniper berries (actually the fleshy female cones) that form a resinous spice used to flavor gin, game meat, and other things. Creeping juniper (*J. horizontalis*) is enormously popular in landscaping, so its foliage comes in bright green, gray-green, yellow, and variegated. It forms a prickly carpet.

Mint belongs to an extensive family of herbs. Mountain mint has several species, including short-toothed mountain mint (*Pycnanthemum muticum*) and hoary mountain mint (*P. incanum*). Both have pale gray-green foliage and white flowers dotted with pink or purple. These are native to New Jersey.

Oregano means "brightness of the mountain," and it grows around much of the Mediterranean and beyond, bearing tiny white flowers and flavorful leaves. Greek mountain oregano (*Oreganum vulgarus*) comes from the mountains of Greece and has an intense spicy taste. Roundleaf oregano (*O. rotundifolium*) has a mounding form and thrives in sunny, rocky, well-drained places.

Rose is a large family of plants, with many fancy modern cultivars. Wild roses do better in rock gardens as they are smaller and tougher. They also tend to produce better hips. Mountain rose (*Rosa woodsii* var. *ultramontana*) is a small, fragrant rose that yields excellent hips for tea and pink rose petals for potpourri. It comes from the Sierra Nevada range.

Sage is a genus with many popular members. Mountain sage (*Salvia regla*) is a fragrant shrub with spectacular scarlet flowers. This drought-tolerant plant attracts hummingbirds. It comes from the rocky slopes of the Chisos Mountains. Clary sage (*S. verbenaca*) is a sprawling herb with bright purple flowers. It has a far-flung range including the British islands, Mediterranean, and Caucasus. Common sage (*S. officinalis*) also does well in rock gardens. It has the best culinary flavor and medicinal popularity.

St. John's wort, or *Hypericum,* is a genus with nearly worldwide distribution. Mountain St. John's wort (*Hypericum montanum*) comes from Eurasia and Morocco. It has cheerful yellow flowers. Common St. John's wort (*H. perforatum*) is used to uplift mood.

Thyme is an herb with various wild and cultivated versions. Mountain thyme (*Thymus praecox* ssp. *arcticus,* syn. *T. serpyllum*) is a mat-forming plant with tiny green leaves and bright pink flowers. It grows wild across much of Europe, including higher elevations. Its 'Elfin' cultivar only grows one to three inches high, forming a nearly flat mat of leaves. Creeping thyme (*T. praecox* 'Coccineus') has glossy green leaves and pink to red flowers. It will fill in space between large rocks. Woolly thyme (*T. praecox* ssp. *britannicus*) has fuzzy gray-green leaves and rarely flowers. It creeps to fill in spaces and roots as it grows, but also trails over edging. For a more upright habit, consider silver thyme (*T. vulgaris* 'Argenteus') with its white-edged leaves or golden lemon thyme (*T. pulegioides* 'Aureus') with yellow lemon-scented leaves.

Yellow gentian (*Gentiana lutea*) is tall for an alpine plant and has yellow flowers. It grows in alpine pastures, preferring calcareous soils with lots of chalk or lime.

Constructing an Alpine Rock Garden

Rock gardens are very flexible in size, so you can suit them to your budget and available space. You can make anything from a miniature container garden to a wall spanning the length of your yard. It is better to start small and build from there. If you want a big garden, consider building it in stages so you can create different microclimates along the way.

First, consider location. Almost all alpines need full sun or close to it. A southern or southwestern exposure works best in most places (reverse in the Southern Hemisphere). A slope is also an asset. If you have one already, use that. If not, you will need to build a sloping garden or wall. However, if you live in a mountainous area, you have the option of just choosing accent stones and planting things in your yard. Using native species will make this very easy.

Alpines require poor, well-drained soil. The easiest way to achieve this is to build up a raised bed or wall. Alternatively, you can dig out soil to make an in-ground rock garden. Lay in a bottom layer of sand or fine gravel. Above that put soil or compost mixed with sand or fine gravel. Refer to the composition required for your intended plants. Avoid rich fertilizers. Decomposed rock is the best amendment for rock gardens as it adds mineral availability without overstocking organic nutrients.

Place boulders so they look natural. You need to bury at least one third of the height and put the widest part on the bottom. This is easier to do by filling from the bottom up than by trying to dig a big hole. Also, physics is your friend! Use levers, ropes, and pulleys to move medium-size rocks. Larger rocks benefit from professionals who can use small landscaping engines like a frontloader to move them. If you have live rock covered in moss or lichen, wrap it in carpet to protect it during the move.

Once you have the soil and boulders in place, add your alpine plants. Choose spacing with care as most grow slowly. You can add a top mulch of gravel or pebbles to discourage weeds and pests, especially if you have mostly miniature shrubs.

A dry stone wall can be built without mortar, and despite what people say today, it is possible to build them surprisingly high that last for quite a long time. The key is how you choose stones—the biggest must go on the bottom, and you have to take time to find a perfect, stable fit for every stone. Layer a little soil between them, tuck in your plants, and add the next layer. A cheaper, slower way is to mix alpine plant seeds into the soil and let them sprout, thus avoiding transplant shock. It is easier to build a retaining wall that leans against a bank of earth than a freestanding wall, but both work for rock gardens.

Conclusion

An alpine rock garden is a lovely little gem. It contrasts the rough stone with the softer plants. If you choose the plants well, it can flower across several seasons. It even grows herbs in a way that naturally concentrates their flavor. Alpine plants are tough little things, and they can enliven an otherwise inhospitable part of the yard. Indoors, a container version lets you recreate a mountaintop in miniature. Turn to your favorite pictures of mountain views and imagine how you could make your own.

Resources

"Alpines & Rock Gardens." Let's Go Gardening. Accessed August 16, 2020. http://www.letsgogardening.co.uk/alpines.htm.

"A Rock Garden or an Alpine Garden?" Greenwood Nursery. Accessed August 16, 2020. https://www.greenwoodnursery.com/blog/rock-garden-or-alpine-garden.

Domoney, David. "How to: build and plant an alpine rock garden," *David Domoney* (blog). Accessed August 16, 2020. https://www.daviddomoney.com/how-to-create-an-alpine-rockery-feature/.

Kowalchik, Claire, and William H. Hylton, eds. *Rodale's Illustrated Encyclopedia of Herbs*. Emmaus, PA: Rodale Press, 1987.

Everything Old Is New Again

✺ Monica Crosson ✺

Some of my best memories are in the garden. My first recollections are of being barefoot and messy-haired and grasping the back of my mother's shirt as she and my grandmother walked through her dahlia bed. I remember looking up (for I was much smaller than the stately plantings) and being taken aback by the loveliness of those impressive blooms. It was my grandfather who introduced me to the habit of growing things. He taught me to be mindful of light and wind patterns, showed me how to plant by the moon phases, and introduced me to seed saving. He also taught me about composting and shared garden folkways associated

with his southern roots. My mother was an artist in the garden. She filled my childhood with gardens that were intimate and whimsical—perfect for the dreamer that I was.

As I grew older, I surrounded myself with friends and mentors who were talented gardeners with varying skills and ideas about what the perfect garden should look like. Some of the gardeners I know specialize in herbs or native plants, while others work strictly with flowers. Some grow only vegetables in a backyard plot, and still others have lovely potted gardens that fill their homes and tumble out onto porches and balconies. As for me, my garden is a modern take on a medieval potager garden. Seventeen raised beds are intermingled with flower beds and rows of blueberries and raspberries, hardy kiwi, patches of herbs, greenhouses, and water features.

It has allowed me to experiment with just about every kind of planting that you can think of, from plants that can be used in the dye pot to medicinal herbs or even plants whose roots dig deep into esoteric practices. Along with my standard favorite "potage" fair, my large garden also allows me to test out new hybrid or interesting heirloom varieties of vegetables, and my flowerbeds are continuously expanding. Through experimenting, I have discovered a few new garden favorites that really aren't that new at all—in fact, some are downright ancient.

Making a Comeback

For years heirloom enthusiasts have worked to resurrect lost garden gems, educate gardeners, and spark within all of us a longing for the nostalgic. Chefs too have rediscovered heirloom and ancient varieties that once bulked-out and sweetened the potage and have elevated them to satisfy our modern palette.

And most recently, the pandemic, which kept us close to home, brought on a new interest in gardening spurred by fears of food shortages. Backyard gardens, community gardens, and victory gardens have been on the rise, causing not only a widespread spike in seed sales but also an interest in the preservation of seed, which can't be done with hybrid varieties.

Hybrid vegetables (also known as F1 hybrid) are plants that resulted from pollination between two genetically distinct plants to create a desired trait. Because they are designed to be used for one season, second-generation plants will yield less or no fruit and may have physical characteristics that vary greatly from first-generation plants. Heirloom varieties, on the other hand, not only boast the ability to save and pass down their seed but are adaptable to regional climate and soil conditions, which improves their hardiness and disease and pest resistance. Most importantly, they have a superior taste and nutritional value you don't find in commercially grown hybrid vegetables.

Old Favorites

Bringing back vegetable varieties that thrived in the past lends a greater diversity of taste and color to the table, helps preserve biodiversity, and provides healthier plants that require less fuss in the garden. So let's take a stroll through a garden where radishes are black and Rapunzel isn't just a girl who was held in a tower. Here heirloom favorites mingle with ancient greens and your taste buds will be happy you took the time to visit.

'Amish Paste' Tomato (*Lycopersicon lycopersicum*)

Dating from the 1800s, this meaty plum variety was brought to us by the Amish of Wisconsin. These tomatoes are the largest of the plum tomatoes, weighing in between eight and twelve ounces each, and are perfect as a slicer or for processing into salsas or sauces. They are known for having sparse foliage, which makes them slightly susceptible to sun scald and cracking. Start seeds indoors four to six weeks weeks before the last frost. Harden off plants by placing them in a sheltered place outdoors for a week before transplanting. Because they are indeterminate in nature, 'Amish Paste' tomatoes should be trellised or caged. They mature in eighty to ninety days.

Black Spanish Radish (*Raphanus sativus*)
A winter variety of the Brassicaceae family, black radishes have been grown in Europe since the 1500s. With three-to-four-inch globes, they have a crisp, spicy flavor that lends well to stir-fries and stews and is an excellent addition to a salad. Black radishes are easy to grow and store well. They boast high amounts of vitamin C as well as vitamins A, E, and B. They are also a good source of iron, magnesium, and potassium. Medicinally, they were once used to improve the gallbladder and for pulmonary health. Direct sow the seeds in late summer for fall or winter use. The radishes mature in fifty-five to seventy days.

Carlin Peas (*Pisum sativum*)
Pease porridge, anyone? Carlin, or Carling, peas are a mealier, more protein-rich legume that was a primary ingredient of the pottage and mushy peas before the eighteenth century. They grow much like a sweet pea on vines that reach up to six feet with pink and purple blooms. Peas are small and brown and can be used fresh or dried. Start indoors six weeks before the last frost date or direct sow in spring after. Typically, there will be seventy days between planting and harvest.

Carlin Pea Hummus

  2 cloves garlic

  2 16-ounce cans Carlin peas, drained and rinsed

  5 tablespoons olive oil, plus 1 tablespoon for garnish

  Juice of 1 lemon

  ¼ cup tahini

  1 teaspoon cumin

  ½ teaspoon paprika

  Salt and pepper to taste

  1 tablespoon chopped fresh parsley

Process garlic cloves in food processor until finely chopped. Add Carlin peas, 5 tablespoons olive oil, lemon juice, tahini, cumin, paprika, and salt and pepper to taste and blend until smooth. Spoon into a bowl and add remaining tablespoon of olive oil and chopped parsley. Serves 4 as a snack.

Good-King-Henry (*Chenopodium bonus-henricus*)

Also known as allgood, fat hen, and goosefoot, Good-King-Henry was a staple of backyard gardens for hundreds of years. And if you practice permaculture, this green is a nice low-maintenance herb to add to your plantings. It grows in both full sun and partial shade and reaches a height of two and half feet tall. Shoots can be harvested in the spring and eaten like asparagus. The leaves, which are said to have a mild spinach flavor, can be gathered all summer and cooked as you would spinach or kale. This perennial plant can be slow to germinate and harvesting shouldn't begin until the third year.

Lovage (*Levisticum officinale*)

This native of the Mediterranean was chewed by ancient Greeks to ease digestion and relieve gas. It came to America with early settlers who would candy the root and chew on the seeds to help keep them stay alert through long church services. Before celery became common, lovage, whose taste is very similar, was eaten as a salad green and used to flavor the pottage. All parts of the plant can be consumed, and it can be used in any dish you would use celery. It is very impressive in the garden, reaching up to six feet in height with bright yellow flowers that are fragrant during the midsummer months. Once established, it requires minimal care.

Rampion (*Campanula rapunculus*)

When the Brothers Grimm published "Rapunzel" in 1812, rampion, or rapunzel, was commonly grown in herb gardens. Native to Europe, Asia, and North Africa, it is a member of the bellflower family. Rampion is a biennial that reaches a height of two to three feet with delicate blue, lilac, or white bell-shaped flowers that bloom in June or July. Young rampion leaves can be eaten in the spring, with a slightly bitter taste. They are high in vitamin C. The fleshy roots can be eaten raw to replace radishes in salads or cooked, providing a nutty flavor to heartier dishes.

Vinaigrette

> 1 finely chopped garlic clove
>
> 1 tablespoon finely chopped shallots
>
> Salt and pepper to taste
>
> 2 teaspoons dijon mustard
>
> 2 tablespoons red wine vinegar
>
> 6 tablespoons olive oil

Rapunzel Salad

    6 cups loosely torn mesclun salad mix

    1 cup young loosely torn rampion leaves

    4–5 rampion roots, cleaned and sliced

    3 ounces crumbled goat cheese

For the vinaigrette, whisk together garlic, shallots, salt and pepper, mustard, and vinegar. Slowly add olive oil and mix. Set aside.

Toss greens and roots and drizzle with desired amount of vinaigrette. To serve, divide among plates and sprinkle with goat cheese. Serves 4.

'Rouge Vif d'Etampes' Pumpkin (*Cucurbita maxima*)

Also known as Cinderella pumpkins, these date back to the 1800s and were a popular French market pumpkin. Not only are they a showstopper in the garden with bright red-orange flesh and reaching weights of up to twenty pounds, they are delicious in recipes and store well. Seeds can be directly sown after the last frost in mounds (three to four seeds per mound), six to eight feet apart.

Skirret (*Sium sisarum*)

Skirret, or crummock, is of Chinese origin and was a dining room staple for hundreds of years across Britain. Eventually it fell out of favor as the easier-to-harvest potatoes and carrots became the norm. Skirret should be sown indoors six to eight weeks before the last frost date or directly sown into the garden after danger of frost has passed. It can also be propagated by root division. Patience is required with skirret, as harvest cannot take place for six to eight months after planting. The good news is that its roots can be harvested directly from the ground all winter as it is extremely cold hardy, so skirret is a wonderful addition to your winter garden. Serve raw in salads or serve in your favorite stews or sautéed in butter.

'Spanish Black' Carrot (*Daucus carota*)

With roots tracing back to Afghanistan, purple carrots were well-known in Europe since the Middle Ages. With purple flesh and a yellow core, this cultivar is high in vitamin C, vitamin B1, and carotenoids. It is a lovely addition to a salad or sautéed dish but can lose its vibrancy when baked. Direct sow carrot seeds in spring in soil that has been loosened to twelve inches deep. Barely cover with one-quarter to one-half inch of soil and water well. Thin out seedlings to approximately eighteen per square foot.

Upland Cress (*Barbarea verna*)

Also known as winter cress or creasy greens, this slow-bolting green is similar to watercress but easier to grow. A native to southwestern Europe and cultivated since the seventeenth century in England, it has naturalized in Asia, Europe, and the United States. With its peppery flavor, it is high in vitamins A, C, K, and B12 as well as potassium, iron, manganese, and calcium, and it can be harvested as a microgreen, as a baby green, or at full size. It's a wonderful addition to a salad or sandwich, used in pesto, and mixed in soups and sauces. It can be planted from mid-spring to late summer by direct sowing a quarter inch deep in well-loosened soil about a half inch apart. Thin to four inches apart and keep well watered. Sow every two weeks for continuous use. Upland cress matures in approximately forty-five days.

Upland Cress Pesto

    ½ cup walnuts

    3 cups loosely packed upland cress

    1 chopped clove garlic

    Zest of 1 lemon

    Coarse salt

    ½ cup grated parmesan cheese

    ½ cup olive oil

Place the nuts in a food processor and pulse until finely ground. Add upland cress, garlic, lemon zest, and salt to taste and pulse until finely chopped. Add cheese to combine. With motor running, slowly pour in oil and process until combined. makes about 2½ cups.

Wethersfield Red Onions (*Allium cepa*)

It was once said Wethersfield onions could pay for anything. Originating in Wethersfield, Connecticut, in the eighteenth century and grown extensively for market during the nineteenth century, Wethersfield shipped out a total of five million pounds per year. This red onion is a large, medium-firm onion that grows flatter than most varieties of red onions, with a pleasant flavor. Plant seeds indoors four to six weeks before the last frost date and transplant as soon as the ground can be worked. Harvest 110 days after planting.

White Scallop Squash (*Cucurbita pepo*)

This unique, white, patty pan–style squash is native to North America and was grown for hundreds of years by Native Americans before being introduced to European settlers in the sixteenth century. It is easy to grow and is excellent grilled, fried, or baked with a thin edible skin. Direct sow after last frost date in mounds (three to four seeds per mound) six to eight feet apart.

Tomato and Squash Relish

> 3 cups quartered favorite heirloom cherry-size tomatoes
>
> 1 white scallop squash cut into ¼-inch pieces
>
> 1 tablespoon olive oil
>
> 2 tablespoons balsamic vinegar
>
> Salt and pepper to taste
>
> ¼ cup julienned basil
>
> ⅛ cup thyme leaves

Combine cut tomatoes and squash. Add olive oil, vinegar, and salt and pepper. Fold in fresh herbs. Set aside for about 30 minutes before serving.

Eye Appeal: Turn Your Herb Garden into a Fairytale Setting

⤜ James Kambos ⤛

Every herb garden begins with a dream. A vision. They say every garden grows three times over. First, in our mind. That's when we "see" the herb garden we hope to have. We can visualize the lavender blooming lavishly. We can see a hummingbird as it alights atop the shaggy flower on a stem of monarda. The second time we grow our herb garden is when we place our seed orders on a snowy winter afternoon. Just for a moment we catch a glimpse in our mind's eye of those seeds sprouting, reaching for the sun on a warm late spring afternoon. The third time we can see our herb garden growing is usually when we are lured outside on a chilly but sunny early spring day. We stand

in our herb garden, or where we hope our herb garden will be. Now we're transported in our mind to our herb garden as it should appear in its mature autumn glory. For a brief moment, we see the silver-green stems of yarrow, topped with their golden flowers. This is when we think we can see the silvery artemisias and their elegant foliage too.

This is also when reality sets in. This is when many of us begin to wonder, how am I going to create that fairytale setting I want my herb garden to have? How do I give my herb garden that eye appeal I've seen so often in magazines?

I know how you feel. It can seem like quite a task to go from creating or redesigning an herb garden in your mind to making it a reality. When I began my herb garden years ago, I only knew two things: I liked herbs and I liked plants. I didn't know how to put it all together to give it a pleasing design, what I call eye appeal. Bit by bit I found my way. I made mistakes and I had successes. It finally came together. Now I'm able to share the lessons I learned to help you create the herb garden you've dreamed of.

Easy Does It

The first advice I give to someone designing an herb garden may sound strange coming from an herb gardener—don't plant anything. Hear me out on this. I love herbs, plants, and flowers as much as anyone could. But it's easy to go into a garden center or plant nursery and get carried away buying this and that. I strongly urge you to not go on a buying frenzy first. You'll end up with some awesome plants perhaps, but without a plan in mind you'll start planting here and there. Then you'll have an unorganized jumble of plants.

You must begin to think like a landscaper, a designer. What kind of herb garden do you want? What kind of mood do you wish your herb garden to evoke? If you aren't sure, look at your home and its interior. The style of your home will likely influence the style of your herb garden.

Is your home contemporary and sleek? Then your herb garden will probably have clean lines and simple plantings. Is your home a traditional Cape Cod? Your herb garden will probably lean to a classic cottage style herb garden, with some climbing roses. If your home is a cabin, then your herb garden design might take a cue from nature. In this case the herb garden will still be planned, but its design will be more natural and casual in feel.

So, before you buy one plant or dig one hole, think mood and style. Take it slow and easy—don't buy or plant everything at once.

As your herb garden grows and evolves, repeat this mantra: *Keep the design in mind.*

Planting Your Dream

By now you probably have your dream herb garden design firmly in your mind. Now you're almost ready to plant the herb garden you've been dreaming of. No matter what you have in mind, whether it'll be an herb garden made up of some raised beds or plots divided by boxwood shrubs and stone paths, there are some basic planting tips used by herbalists and garden designers I've known that you should consider.

To begin with, try to avoid planting an herb garden with an overwhelming variety of herbs planted with only one or two specimens of each. This will give you a cluttered look.

Try to focus on a theme. You might consider focusing on a certain type or a shape of foliage. Or you may stick with certain scents, such as lemon/citrus, for example. Or you may decide on herbs with silver and blue-green foliage. Another idea is planting herbs with only pink and blue flowers. Just select a theme and stick with it. You might also consider a different theme for different beds. This achieves a pleasant look too.

Once you've selected your theme, plant large clumps of the same herb. Usually in clumps of three; more if you have the space is fine. Planting in this manner will give you broad sweeps of color, foliage, and fragrance.

Naturally, you'll want to plant ground cover herbs in front of the border, or between stepping-stones for two reasons. First, a ground cover will soften the edges of a straight border as it spills over and onto a garden path, or the side of a raised bed. Second, when a ground cover herb such as thyme is planted between stepping-stones, as it's stepped on, it will release a most delightful scent.

Massing your herbs in the manner I've described throughout your herb garden beds and borders will give you a carpet of color, foliage, and fragrance. Remember, it's more desirable to plant a few herbs in large groups, rather than many single herbs scattered all about.

Take It to the Next Level

Since most herbs are low growing, it's a good idea to break up the mass of herbs by introducing some height here and there. This serves as a nice "pause" among the lower growing plants and gives the viewer's eye a break. Adding height in the herb garden may be done by using some taller-growing plants or by adding a man-made feature.

Here are some ways to add height to the herb garden. I'll start with plants.

Taller perennials are an easy way to bring height to the herb garden. You might consider something like peonies. Blooming in the spring, they'll bring early luscious color to the herb garden. When the flowers fade, you'll still have attractive foliage on two-foot stems. Another good choice is Asiatic lilies. These late-spring bloomers come in an array of colors and add elegance to the herb border on stems up to three and a half feet tall. For just summer color, you may want to try cleome. Blooming in white or pink, cleome carries its flowers on sturdy four-foot stems. Cleomes are annuals that self-seed.

Plant the most fragrant herbs along the edge of a path or in front of a border. Then as you walk past, you'll brush them and release their scent.

Small trees such as dogwoods and Japanese maples add height to an herb garden without overwhelming it. They'll also give dappled shade and a sense of calm.

If you're looking for a man-made element to use as a tall focal point in the herb garden, consider an obelisk (tuteur) or an arch. They add architectural interest and can be used with or without a vine growing on them.

Final Touches

Once you have the herb garden planted, it's time to add some finishing touches. These finishing touches should say something about you. They may include decorative accents such as potted plants, benches, statuary, or perhaps garden gazing globes. I'm sure you'll have other ideas of your own. Here are my thoughts about these decorative items I've mentioned.

Potted plants are lovely additions to any herb garden for several reasons. They can serve to highlight a certain plant and give it importance. They can add seasonal color to the border. Potted plants can also define a corner of a patio or the beginning of a path.

Items such as benches or gazing globes can serve as a centerpiece. They can also give the garden a visual break from only plants.

Statues should be discreet and not over the top. A small statue tucked among the herbal foliage is charming and adds a sense of fantasy to the herb garden.

Have fun experimenting with your decorative final touches until you get the look you want.

———

Hopefully my ideas will help you create not just an herb garden but a sanctuary you can enjoy for years to come.

Plant Identification Skills and Resources

≫ Lupa ≪

It's a late summer morning, and I am walking through my backyard to the lake beyond. My feet brush against hairy cat's ear and pearly everlasting, picking up the damp of last night's rain. I walk past one of the enormous fuschia bushes planted here years ago by the previous owner of the property, its bright pink flowers visited by Anna's hummingbirds. As I approach the lake, I can smell the pungent scent of tall Sitka spruce and western hemlock trees, and I pick berries from the evergreen huckleberry and salal bushes that grow in their shade. By the water's edge, yellow pond lily and water hemlock, their flowers long since gone to seed, soak up as much of the summer sun

as they can, and tiny leaves of duckweed proliferate on the water's surface. Further out, I look to see if any invasive Brazilian elodea or Eurasian watermilfoil show tendrils under the surface in spite of efforts to control their spread.

These are just a few of the plants that I encounter on a two-minute walk through my rural backyard. I'm an amateur naturalist, a generalist who loves to explore all layers of biology, geology, hydrology, and other studies that add up to my favorite: ecology. That doesn't make plant identification a piece of cake for me every time, of course. But it's an important skill to have, whether your interest in plants is magical, herbal, culinary, scientific, leisurely, or some combination thereof. There's joy in being able to find something edible out in the woods and fields or knowing that a particular plant may be able to help with an ailment or a spell. (I also love the minor triumph I feel when someone I'm with asks "What's this plant?" and I'm able to correctly identify it.)

There are lots of plants out there that can be harmful or even fatal if ingested; others can cause a nasty rash or allergic reaction. Never, ever touch or especially eat any plant unless you are 200 percent sure you know exactly what it is and that it's safe. If it's something you personally have never encountered, be prepared for an allergic or other reaction anyway, just in case.

I'd like to discuss some of the skills and resources you can use for plant identification, particularly if you're a beginner. This should not be considered an exhaustive guide to botany but a layperson's starter kit.

Observation

The first skill involves being able to pay attenti[on]
about the plant. Here are a few questions to get y[ou]

- Is it a plant with a wood trunk and branches ...
  a shrub, an herb (a non-woody annual plant), a grass, or
  some other sort of plant?

- How big is it, and how is the plant shaped overall?

- Does it have one or several trunks or stems, and how are
  the branches or smaller stems arranged on it?

- How big are the leaves (including needles), what color
  are they, how are they shaped (including the edges), and
  how are they arranged on the stem? Are they flat and dry
  or thick and fleshy?

- Are there flowers, seeds, or cones? Look at colors, shapes,
  and whether they are found singly or in clusters.

- If it is a woody plant, what does the bark look like? What
  color is it, and how rough is it? If you notice trees that
  look like they may be the same species (similar leaves)
  but different ages, see if the bark looks different on a
  younger tree versus an older one. If you have paper and a
  pencil or crayon, try making a bark rubbing.

- If you are able to observe the roots without hurting
  the plant, is there a single taproot or just a network of
  smaller roots?

- Do you notice multiple plants connected to each other
  by rhizomes (a long stemlike structure that travels horizontally along the ground)?

Now look at the habitat the plant is in:

Joes it seem to prefer sun, shade, or somewhere in between? If you see the plant species in both sun and shade, does one population seem happier and healthier than the other?

- What is the soil like? Is it damp or dry? Dark or light? Claylike, sandy, or similar to the soil in your garden?

- Is there water nearby, including groundwater? Does the plant prefer being closer to water, or does it even grow only right next to or in it?

- Is the plant well sheltered from wind and weather, or is it exposed when storms and other weather patterns come through?

- Do you see many animals, including insects and other small invertebrates, nearby? Do you see any signs that animals have been feeding on the plant?

Pay attention to seasonal cues too. Note what time of year it is, and pay attention to whether the plant has visible leaves, flowers, cones, seeds, or other seasonal features. Even color changes can be indicative of season; many conifers, for example, grow new bunches of needles in the spring that are a lighter color than older needles.

Do your best to collect as much information as you can. You can even write it down in a field journal if you like. Take pictures if you have your phone or a camera too. If you like to draw, you can make sketches of it in the field. Be cautious about taking samples, especially if you don't see very many individual plants of this species or if you aren't sure whether it's something that could cause an allergic reaction or other skin rash.

Taking a Second Look

Now that you have gathered information, it's time to use it to figure out what sort of plant you've found. This is a good time to take a second, closer look at the plant's details to see if there's anything you overlooked the first time around.

Let's look at leaves as one example. During warmer months, one of the easiest ways to identify deciduous plants is by their leaves. Some of the things you'll want to pay attention to are the following:

- The size and overall shape of the leaf, particularly as similar-looking leaves may mainly be differentiated by size.

- What the edges look like. Are they smooth, wavy, lobed, serrated? If serrated, are all the "teeth" the same size, or are some smaller than others?

- How many leaves are on one stem? If there's more than one, are they arranged in one big cluster, or are they in pairs along the stem? If in pairs, are they right across from each other, or do they alternate along the stem? Do they get smaller toward the end of the stem away from the branch, or are all the leaves basically the same size?

- What is the texture like? Smooth, rough, leathery, fleshy, hairy, spiny, waxy, or some combination thereof?

- How are the veins arranged? Is there one central vein with others branching off? If so, do those branching veins have smaller, branching veins as well? Are the branching veins in matched pairs, or do they alternate? Or, instead of all those branching veins, does the leaf have several parallel veins that run along the entire length of the leaf?

But what if your plant is a conifer tree of some sort, with needles instead of deciduous leaves? Well, you can still go into detail on that? Here are some starting points:

- Again, the overall size and shape are important; some conifers have short, bristly needles while others have longer, elegant ones. Note the shape of needle clusters, and whether the needles all point in generally the same direction or whether they form a whorl or bunch. Are the needles arranged all the way around the stem, in two lines to create a "flat" look, or some other arrangement?

- How many needles are in one individual bundle? White pines in North America, for example, generally have bundles of five needles, while yellow pines have two or three.

- What color are the needles? Are they a deep forest green or more of a blue tone, for example?

- Are the tips of the needles really sharp or more rounded and blunt?

- Pick a needle, roll it in your fingers like a pencil, and, if possible, neatly cut it in half. What shape is the cross section? Is it a triangle, a diamond, or some other shape?

Leaves and needles are just one example of physical characteristics that can be very helpful in plant identification. You can do the same thing with looking at the other details I mentioned in the first section, such as looking in more detail at how the flowers are put together or how branches grow off the main stem or trunk. Some of this you'll learn to recognize as you collect more plant identifications and start to familiarize yourself with common patterns, but if you want to really get detailed about it, check out *Botany in a Day* by Thomas J. Elpel.

Time for Identification!

Now that you've gotten all the information you can about the plant, it's time to figure out what it is! There are a number of resources available to you to help:

Field Guides

These books carry a wealth of information about plants and how to identify them. In many places you can get general field guides that talk about the plants in a given country or region; in the United States there are many places where you can get field guides that talk about plants specifically in your state or even a particular biome within your state (such as a coastline or mountains). I like having a variety of them on hand, and while I prefer those with photos, there are also some with nice, detailed illustrations. Most will also give information like maps of where the plants are typically found, typical size, when they usually flower, and so on.

There are a few ways to use a field guide. I like to just flip through until I see something that looks like what I saw and bookmark it, then keep going. If you think you might know what sort of plant you have, you can skip ahead to that section to see. As you get more experienced, you may be able to guess what family or even genus the plant is in and use that to narrow down your search.

I always check my research in multiple books. If I think I know the identification, I look up that species in every applicable field guide and in other resources too, just to be sure. And I'm always open to being wrong.

Websites and Other Online Resources

My favorite way to use the internet for identification is to simply type descriptive words into any good search engine (I like Ecosia, personally) and then check the results, especially images. For example, I might type in "red berries on Oregon coast" to get myself started, and then see if any of the pictures look like what I saw. Or I may look for "conifers of California," and often among the first few websites that come up will be a site that shows pictures and information about some of or all the conifers found in that state.

I also really like Facebook groups and Reddit subreddits if I want to ask other people their opinions. One of my favorite groups on Facebook is called "Plant Identification: The Afterparty," and I also like r/whatsthisplant on Reddit. Make sure you post at least one good, clear picture; it's better to have multiple pictures, to include close-ups of details like leaves, and also at least one picture of the whole plant if possible. Mention where you saw it as well.

Identification Apps

These are my secret weapon! They're a great way to enter in a picture of a plant and get suggestions on what they might be. My favorite one is iNaturalist, a free app for both iPhones and Android phones. Not only does it use algorithms that draw on millions of user observations to compare your photo to other plants found in your area, but other users can look at your picture and tell you what they think it is. (You can do that for others too as you get more experienced.) And best of all, if another user verifies your identification, that observation is now research-grade, which means scientists can use it in their research!

Human Resources

Don't be afraid to call or email nearby people who might be able to help. If you have a botany, biology, or other natural sciences department at a nearby college or university, someone there may be able to help you figure out an identification for your plant. Try contacting your local university cooperative extension. State and federal parks, wildlife refuges, and other natural resource centers also often have biologists on staff.

These are just some of the resources that are available to you. You may find you gravitate toward some over others, and that's okay!

Telling Similar Plants Apart

There are times when you may have trouble telling the difference between two very similar species. Sometimes it's the smallest differences that can let you know whether you've found toxic poison hemlock or edible Queen Anne's lace, for example.

The first thing to do is to take a close look at the details of both species and see if you notice anything that differentiates them. For example, poison hemlock has purple spots on the stem while Queen Anne's lace does not. Hemlock's flower clusters are more spread out than the other's, and it grows much larger.

Your field guides and other resources may have explanations on how to tell a given plant from its lookalike; just look up the potential species and see if lookalikes are mentioned. Make sure you really familiarize yourself with as many dangerous plants in your area as possible so that you recognize them when you see them.

When in doubt, try asking other people! More experienced botanists, naturalists, herbalists, and the like are often happy to help you figure out what you have and explain what to look for.

———

Again, this is just a very short beginner's guide to plant identification. Check out the resources I've mentioned throughout, and you are also always welcome to contact me at lupa.green wolf@gmail.com if you need further resources.

The Purposeful and Practical Colonial Garden

ᜒ Marilyn I. Bellemore ᜑ

O ne of the perks of growing up in New England was the abundance of museums and historic sites. As a child, I knew that after touring a prominent homestead, I would have the chance to get a stick of rock candy or trinket from the gift shop and then do my favorite thing: wander outdoors in the Colonial garden. As a youngster, these gardens were plots of magnificent beauty for me. But over time, I learned that they were also a family's main food source and medicine cabinet.

In Colonial times, herbs, flowers, vegetables, and certain fruits were most often planted together in narrow raised beds that were either square or rectangular in shape so everything grown was easy to reach. Ambitious Colonists used traditional wooden fencing or more aesthetically pleasing shrubbery around the borders to keep hungry critters at bay. It also helped as protection against the wind and unpredictable weather.

Planting, tending to, and harvesting the garden was generally the responsibility of women and children. Often called "kitchen gardens," they were situated within close proximity to the home for convenience. At the many museums I've visited, they've been located in both the front and back yards.

To me, thoughts of early America brings to mind Plymouth Colony, Massachusetts, and its lore states that the Pilgrims transported seeds to the United States from Europe in 1620. However, their first planting season was a failure. After they formed a relationship with the Native Americans, the following year proved fruitful in that the Colonists were taught how to garden the New England soil and adapt to the climate, which was quite different from their homeland. Although weather dependency was an issue, they learned that by adding manure and patches of straw to the soil, the compost would produce heat and lengthen the growing season.

Back then, having a garden was a necessity for survival, whereas modern gardens focus more on pleasure or luxury. Everything in the Colonial garden served a purpose, from the vegetables the Colonists ate to the flowers that were grown for consumption and medicinal reasons, rather than a decorative vaseful on a kitchen table.

My own garden is a fun hobby. I like to see what grows best in the mountains of central Vermont, and each year, I add new vegetables and herbs to the mix. Sometimes I incorporate popular items that would be grown in a Colonial garden, such as calendula and rue. When it comes to taking care of my garden, it's second nature for me to go to the local hardware store or nursery for watering cans, hoses, and digging tools.

The Iron Act (1750) caused anger and resentment among the Colonists. The British Crown wanted to limit the Colonists' possession of metal because it could be repurposed for the manufacture of weaponry. Hence, gardening tools were often coveted and stolen. The Iron Act underscored the need for the Colonists to be independent.

For the Colonists, gardening was often a source of stress. Water had to be carried from ponds or streams, which could be far away. In addition, gardening tools were essentials and hard to come by. The earliest rudimentary shovels were handmade from wood. Imagine digging through rocky New England terrain with one. Even with the invention of iron shovels, they still wore out of shape through years of hard use.

I think a commonality between the Colonists and someone such as myself is that through many hours of hard work, the garden was and is a source of pride. Let's take a look at things you might find in a Colonial garden that are long since gone or still here today.

Herbs

Not So Common

Herbs, either fresh or dried, were used to flavor and preserve foods, as dyes, and to scent the home.

Now considered a weed, **purslane** was a popular medicinal herb used to prevent urinary tract infections and diarrhea. It is rich in vitamin C and beta-carotene. The taste is similar to spinach and was used in soups and stews. It was also known as a salad green.

Tansy was a popular insect repellent much like citronella. Colonists used the herb to eliminate parasites within their bodies. It has a bitter taste and is rarely used in cooking today. It was made into tea to alleviate cramps and colic. Tansy's beautiful yellow color made it a popular dye for wool. Because of its pungent smell, it was placed in Colonial coffins to hide odors during body viewings. Do not consume, as it is thought to have toxic properties.

Celandine was once used to treat scurvy and is loaded with vitamin C. Today, it is advised for external use only in the treatment of warts and hemorrhoids.

Rue had many uses. It helped keep animals out of the garden, was used as an insecticide, and also was mixed into a paste to treat dog bites. But at the same time, some people were allergic to the herb and had a reaction like that of poison ivy.

Similar to rue, the weed **plantain** (*Plantago*, not to be confused with the banana-like fruit) was used by Colonists who made it into a poultice to help soothe and heal open wounds. As a tea, it helps constipation, diarrhea, and urinary tract infections.

Common

Still true today, the lovely fragrance of **lavender** provided a fresh, clean scent for the home along with soothing qualities. It was used in teas, sachets, and tinctures to treat headaches.

Along with lavender, **bayberry**'s magnificent scent made it a popular deterrent of stinky smells. Its aroma alleviated sinus ailments because it helped shrink the mucous membrane. Bayberry also served as a food preservative. I associate bayberry with the old-fashioned candles I love to buy in museum gift shops. The Colonists reserved bayberry candles for special occasions during the Yuletide season.

Sage has been popular since ancient times, especially during the Roman Empire. There's an old folk belief that says the herb increases longevity and wards off evil spirits. It was used to flavor foods, jellies, and teas, including a sore throat remedy. Sage was also an effective preservative.

Chamomile tea was thought to relieve depression and is still used for its calming properties. Adding the herb to one's bathwater was a welcome remedy for sore, aching muscles and joints. Its petals were used to create a light dye.

Lemon balm is in the mint family, and I always grow mints together in my garden. It was a staple in Colonial gardens. Its furniture polish smell adds a refreshing scent to any home. Lemon balm was used in cakes, cookies, and puddings, and it also flavored meats. It's such a versatile herb that it was also popular as a flavoring for drinks and was used in beauty routines of the time.

Vegetables

Colonists grew heirloom vegetables, meaning that the seeds were saved and then grown over a period of time. It's important to note that seed companies in the United States began after the Revolutionary War. So the saving of seeds was due to their lack of availability, not a measure of frugality.

Along with herbs, the vegetable section of a Colonial garden is my favorite. Corn, squash, beans, cabbage, kale, leeks, pumpkins, turnips, parsnips, and onions are some of what was grown that created a cornucopia of color. Meals were cooked in a large metal kettle over a fireplace, and the women of the family were known to get up as early as 4 a.m. to prepare food for the day ahead.

These healthy and hearty veggies were served with lamb, pork, beef, fish, and chicken on the side or cooked with those meats in soups and stews. The family's main meal was eaten at midday.

Two items you wouldn't find on the Colonial dinner table were broccoli and tomatoes (a fruit called a vegetable by many nutritionists), as they weren't introduced until the nineteenth and twentieth centuries, respectively.

Fruits

There are a couple of facts that I find interesting about fruits and the Colonial garden. Apple, plum, mulberry, peach, and nectarine trees were all around during that time and were planted in orchards. However, if they would fit, Colonists would put fruit trees in the kitchen garden. They were resourceful enough to take the cuttings or roots of fruits and berries that grew wild and replant them in their gardens as well. Melons were also found there.

Fruits were eaten fresh, stewed, and dried. They were made into compotes, tarts, and pies.

Flowers

Nasturtium's beautifully colored flowers made them a delight to look at among the herbs and vegetables. The flower buds and leaves were added to salads and also used like capers. With a somewhat peppery taste, the seeds were harvested to use in pickling recipes.

Like nasturtium, **clove pink** flowers were eaten in salads and sandwiches. They were infused into syrups and vinegars and also made into wines and jams. Dried flowers were added to potpourri to scent linens and the home.

Violets were always the first flowers that I picked as a child growing up in Rhode Island as winter turned to spring. The desirable scent made the flowers a favorite of the Colonists in potpourri and perfumes. They helped with sore throats and persistent coughs. Even today, violets are used to scent skin tonics. They are edible and were sugared with other flowers. I've used them to decorate cakes and have added them dried to exfoliating body scrubs that I enjoy making.

Calendula was extremely popular because the flowers could be eaten, used in medicinal and beauty recipes, and used to create a lovely yellow-greenish dye. Calendula was made into an ointment to stop bleeding and to heal wounds. It was successful in treating bee stings and rubbed into the skin to promote circulation and for its soothing qualities.

Receipts (That's *Recipes* in Colonial Times!)

Plantain Poultice

A friend of mine was recently bitten multiple times by white-faced hornets, so much so that his arm, from fingertips to elbow, was swollen. It itched as much as poison ivy. A neighbor introduced him to a Colonial remedy that provided immediate relief. You can do this too. Pick a couple of plantain leaves (*Plantago*), chew them up, then spit the result onto the affected area. Rub gently and let it dry. Rinse it off after you feel the soothing result.

Violet Tincture

Alcohol was a readily available drink for Colonists. Amazingly, hard ciders, ales, apple brandy, wine, and whiskey were consumed daily. Clean water was often hard to come by, and it was believed to make people sick. Even children drank "small beer," which had a low alcohol content.

Drinking aside, alcohol was an important ingredient when making tinctures. Herbs and flowers were dissolved in rum or whiskey, and the result could be taken on the tongue as a medicinal remedy.

Here's an easy violet tincture that among its many uses soothes throat ailments and treats insect bites. Take any size sterilized mason jar and fill it at least halfway with fresh violets. Cover the flowers with brandy. Seal the jar tightly and put it in a cool, dark place for 4 to 6 weeks. Strain and discard the flowers. Pour the liquid into dropper bottles. Keep and share!

Lemon Balm Tea for Bloating, Gas, or Indigestion

When I make my tea infusions for jellies, I always use fresh herbs. Whenever I can, I do the same for making hot and iced teas. For this recipe, take 1 to 2 handfuls of fresh lemon balm. Put it into a mason jar or metal pitcher and pour in boiling water. Allow to sit for at least 15 minutes then strain and discard the lemon balm. Drink hot in a mug or cold in a glass. Add sugar to taste.

Resources

Bacon, Richard M. *The Forgotten Art of Growing, Gardening and Cooking with Herbs*. Dublin, NH: Yankee, 1972.

Bunney, Sarah. *The Illustrated Encyclopedia of Herbs: Their Medicinal and Culinary Uses*. New York: Dorset, 1992.

Starting a Food Pantry Garden

≫ Kathy Martin ≪

One of my greatest pleasures in growing a vegetable garden is sharing food with others. I love to plant with abandon, filling all the space I have, and give the food to my friends, neighbors, or a food pantry. Sometimes I set up a little table by my mailbox and put my extras there with a sign that says "Free Organic Vegetables from My Garden." They usually disappear fast.

This year I have gone full steam ahead with giving. A group of gardening friends and I set up a company and are farming about a quarter acre with another one and a half acres to expand into. We are an all-volunteer nonprofit organization, and about fifteen volunteers currently work our field. We have rows of tomatoes, squash, potatoes, eggplants, okra, cucumbers, carrots, onions, beets, kale, lettuce, chard, broccoli, cabbage, and more. Just about every vegetable, I think. All our produce is donated to a large local food pantry that has food distribution programs in several nearby towns. It feels good to deliver boxes of fresh vegetables to the pantry. We are harvesting about 100 pounds of food a week as I write and expect to donate 1,500 pounds of food by the end of the year!

We started planning our pantry last winter, before COVID-19 was an issue. Now food security has become a serious problem. In the pandemic economy, nearly one in four US households has not had enough food to eat, reports NPR. The *New York Times* writes that "more than 37 million Americans are food insecure" according to USDA data. Resulting mainly from food chain disruptions and loss of incomes, people face food insecurity that is not only a shortage of food but a lack of nutritious food. Food banks are supposed to fill in the gaps, but with COVID-19 restrictions limiting distribution channels (for example, some indoor pantries have had to close or change to delivery or outdoor distribution) and with the suddenly increased need, food banks are not able to keep up. As a gardener with time and skills to share, I feel it is important to help provide food at a local level.

How to Start a Food Pantry Garden

The simplest way to start a food pantry garden is to repurpose land that you may have into a vegetable garden. Up the street from me, homeowners with a large front lawn have dug out eight or ten long rows and are growing vegetables. I do not know if it is for their own use, but it is nice and big and could be a pantry garden. I am thinking it could be a family project to grow food for donation.

Another pantry garden I have seen work well is in a community garden plot. For this garden, the annual fee was waived by management. The gardeners were a group of students from the local high school with a small grant from the school and advice from an experienced gardener. The students alternated days to weed, plant, water, and harvest. They grew tomatoes, peppers, potatoes, kale, Swiss chard, squash, and green beans. Once a week, they brought their harvest to the local food pantry. This was such a great way for the students to learn about growing vegetables, to get their volunteer credits from their school, to get outside and enjoy the earth, and to give nutritious food to people in need.

*Keys to starting a pantry garden are volunteers,
land, a local pantry, and source of funding.*

I have also seen a pantry garden set up at a community supported agriculture (CSA) farm. An enthusiastic group of experienced gardeners were given a couple of unused beds at the side of the CSA field to cultivate. They funded the project themselves as a group. Costs were minimal since they raised their own seedlings at home and the farm irrigated their beds and provided compost and mulch. By asking the local pantry, the gardeners learned that the community preferred basic garden fare, nothing unusual. They grew carrots, onions, garlic, beets, lettuce, potatoes, squash, tomatoes, sweet peppers, and green beans.

The key pieces to starting a pantry garden are (1) gathering volunteers to tend the garden, including people with gardening knowledge who can lead the project; (2) finding land to cultivate with a source of water for irrigation; (3) identifying a local pantry that needs fresh food and a way to transport the food to it; and (4) finding a source of funding.

Volunteers are the keystone of the project. A successful food pantry garden will require a group of passionate and energetic people with time to work the soil and the ability to organize themselves and work together. It is important to have at least one person with a strong knowledge of gardening or farming who can be a leader and a teacher. Volunteers can be recruited from local garden groups, your neighbors and friends, and local schools.

Land for cultivating is often available with some searching. Ideas range from your own front yard to a field owned by a town or individual who wants it to be kept under cultivation. By contacting local conservation departments and land use groups, you can find land that might be appropriate. Things to consider when selecting where to grow include accessibility of the area for parking and hauling supplies in and produce out, adequate sunlight and fertile, workable soil, a source of water for irrigation, and a nearby place for storing materials and seedlings.

Identifying a local pantry that needs fresh produce is the easy part this year. In past years, pantries in some areas had an overabundance of donated fresh food. With COVID-19, that has changed. Unfortunately, some food pantries have had to shut down because they operated in public buildings that have been closed or could not provide COVID safety for volunteers needed to run the organization. Pantries operating since the pandemic began have had to adapt and might be open air, drive-through operations or might deliver donated food to those in need.

And last but not least is finding a funding source. You will need to scope out your project and project the costs you will have. A small plot at a home or at a community garden may not have major costs, but you will still need seeds and seedlings, compost, fertilizer, mulch, and garden tools. Volunteers can be asked to donate these or contribute money for purchasing them. Or a local organization may be able to sponsor your group. A large pantry garden may have significant costs. An open field may need fencing, irrigation equipment, storage structures, a tractor, mulch, and many seeds and seedlings. In this case, funding sources include soliciting donors with outreach programs, holding fundraising events like plant sales and raffles, and applying for grants.

There are several organizations that can help you with starting a donation garden, and university extension programs also offer great advice:

- Ample Harvest: ampleharvest.org/food-growers
- Plant a Row for the Hungry: https://www.foodgatherers .org/?module=Page&sID=plant-a-row-for-the-hungry
- Michigan State University: canr.msu.edu/news/donate _excess_produce_from_your_garden_to_food_banks _and_food_pantries
- Iowa State University: extension.iastate.edu/ffed /community-donation-gardening-toolkit/

Legal Steps and Hard Work

The donation garden that I am part of is organized as a long-term, professional venture. We are an enthusiastic group of people, one of whom has a wealth of farming experience. We include a retired scientist (me), a retired lawyer, a librarian, and a horticulturalist. By working through our contacts, we found a piece of land that suited our needs. This is owned by a landowner who wants to keep it under cultivation and has gifted the land to us to farm in exchange for a basket of vegetables every week. It is a two-acre field that was previously used for farming for many years. Since the landowner required us to have insurance, we incorporated as a company. Once we did that, we applied for official nonprofit status as a 501(3)(c) company. This is an expensive venture. We worked with a lawyer and, for a total of about $3,000, were awarded nonprofit status from the IRS with permission to solicit funds from the state. This process took us a couple of months to complete and was a fair amount of work.

After finding land and setting up our company, our next challenge was to get the field ready for gardening. Step one was to set up a fence to keep the deer out. We put up a solar electric fence. We fenced in a manageable part of the field to begin with—a 100-by-100-foot plot (about a quarter of an acre). Step two was plowing the field. We rented a rototiller and turned the soil. Next, we installed an irrigation system. Like the previous farmer, we put a pump in the river nearby and ran irrigation lines down each row of our garden. With that done, we scattered organic fertilizer, hand-worked the rows where we would plant, and laid down weed-block fabric. After this, we were ready to plant.

This year we have planted several thousand seedlings—90 percent of these our volunteers have grown at home. We began planting seeds in February. Onion seeds first, then cabbages and broccoli, followed by lots of tomatoes, peppers, eggplant, and a few okra plants. Finally, we planted squashes, cucumbers, and melons. Once our field was ready to plant, we were a bit late in the season, but we got the plants in: two 60-foot rows of cabbage seedlings, three rows of 130 tomato seedlings, at least 100 each eggplants and peppers, three rows of onion seedlings, three of summer squashes, and one of cucumbers. We direct seeded several rows of carrots, parsnips, potatoes, and two patches of corn. Other crops included Swiss chard, lettuce, bok choy, basil, brussels sprouts, broccoli, and kale. We planned to plant escarole, turnips, bulb fennel, radishes, garlic, and more cabbages, broccoli, dill, cilantro, and greens in the fall.

Our first harvest was a celebration for us. In late July, we began picking cabbages, eggplant, and basil. Only a few pounds to start, but by late August we were donating 100 pounds of vegetables a week. As I write, it is October and we have just celebrated crossing the 1,000-pound mark. We are donating all our vegetables to a nearby pantry that serves local towns. This pantry cooks meals for delivery and provides grocery bags of food for drive-up distribution, both new programs this year to accommodate COVID-19 safety.

Challenges

Everything has been a learning experience for us this first year—especially in the garden. We had every type of local wildlife come by and sample our crops. Rabbits ate many young cabbage seedlings, so we lowered the bottom wire of our electric fence and sprayed regularly with rabbit repellant. Turkeys came in and ate bok choy and took dust baths in the middle of rows of tiny carrot and parsnip seedlings. Deer somehow got through our fence and ate a row of lettuce—an extra row of wire on the fence seems to be keeping them out now.

The insects shared our produce too. We had cabbage worms in the broccoli and lost that crop. Tomato hornworms did a fair amount of damage. We had windstorms that knocked down tomato poles and blew peppers off the plants. We had an unusually early frost that damaged the squashes and tomatoes. And the weeds! We had a constant battle. We laid down weed-block fabric, which is expensive for a large field. We ended up mulching extensively with old hay.

We have also worked through challenges with management, fundraising, and finding more volunteers. For fundraising, we first set up a website (aureliasgarden.org) with a donate button and then did a few social media fundraisers. We applied for a state grant (that we have been awarded!). Now we are in the process of putting together an annual appeal letter, applying for more grants, and planning a spring plant sale. We have a budget set for next year, a finance committee, and a fundraising committee in place. I am sure we will be busy all winter.

Next year we are looking forward to building on our experiences. We will expand our space to double the current size. We have plans in place using sustainable practices to reduce weed growth and enrich the soil. We will get our plantings in earlier and plant crops that have done well for us this year. Our projection is that we can increase our food donation by several-fold.

It feels good to be donating food. It also feels great to be out working in the field with a group of volunteers.

Resources

Kenneally, Brenda Ann. "America at Hunger's Edge." *New York Times Magazine*, September 2, 2020. https://www.nytimes.com/interactive/2020/09/02/magazine/food-insecurity-hunger-us.html.

Silva, Christianna. "Food Insecurity in the US by the Numbers." NPR, September 27, 2020. https://www.npr.org/2020/09/27/912486921/food-insecurity-in-the-u-s-by-the-numbers.

Crystals and Cow Horns: Adventures in Biodynamic Gardening

⤞ Melissa Tipton ⤝

I remember, as a teenager, meeting a boy who went to a Waldorf school. At the time, I hadn't a clue what this was (something to do with that weird salad, perhaps?), but as he enthusiastically described a typical day in his high school life, filled with cool science experiments, poetry discussions, and painting theater sets, my own school experience seemed drearily rote in comparison. Thus, my fascination with Rudolf Steiner, whose educational philosophy inspired the Waldorf model, was sparked. (Waldorf Boy was also quite cute, which *might* have had an influence.)

Rudolf Steiner (1861–1925) was the founder of anthroposophy (try saying *that* five times fast), a spiritual movement aimed at enhancing people's ability to perceive the spirit world, with a focus on studying this realm with the same rigor and precision as any scientific investigation. Steiner believed that by increasing their intuitive perception, people would be better equipped to evaluate spiritual teachings for themselves, making them less reliant on external authorities.

This progressive development of intuitive faculties was seen as a necessary evolution of consciousness, with the goal of helping people find a balance between opposing, or polar, influences, sometimes personified as Lucifer and his counterpart, Ahriman. Interestingly, neither figure was seen as wholly good or bad, and their influence became problematic only when there was a lopsided tendency to favor one over the other. Steiner believed harmony was attained by striking a balance between these two extremes, a dynamic that makes an appearance in his take on farming, as we'll see shortly.

The core anthroposophical principles were applied to a variety of fields, such as medicine, architecture, and the arts, and their application to agriculture gave rise to Steiner's unique flavor of organic farming, known as **biodynamic agriculture**. In addition to what one might expect to find in organic methods (avoidance of synthetic chemicals, emphasis on soil health and fertility, etc.), Steiner also incorporated astrological timing; a unique take on composting, which I'll explain how to do in this article; and the use of crystals. He viewed the soil, plants, and animals as a single living system, and the biodynamic approach sought to restore ecological harmony by taking into account not only the terrestrial influences but the cosmic as well.

Rather than battling against nature, biodynamic agriculture aims to partner with the farm ecosystem by, for example, using the collective power of species diversity to control disease and insects; improving soil health with livestock manure, composting, and crop rotation; and controlling weed invasion through mulching and the proper timing of planting. Did I also mention the cow horns stuffed with powdered quartz crystal?

Cow Horn Preparations

One of the key practices of biodynamic agriculture is a series of special preparations, each denoted by a number, 500 through 508, designed to boost soil fertility and plant health, while harmonizing terrestrial and cosmic energies.

Horn Manure

The first preparation, 500, also known as "horn manure," is made by taking fresh manure from lactating cows, removing any straw or other plant material, and packing the manure into a cow's horn. The bony core of the horn must first be removed by letting the horn sit in the sun or a compost pile for a week, at which point the outer "shell" should be easy to slide away from the core.

Once filled with manure, the horn is placed in a carefully sited hole in the ground, away from tree roots and excessively wet areas, with the horn's opening facing downward to prevent water from entering. The pit should be marked for retrieval of the horn, which is done six months later in the Northern Hemisphere or as soon as four months in the Southern. The resultant material should smell rich and humusy, but if it's still wet or smells of manure, it can be reburied.

The timing of this preparation, as with all biodynamic methods, is important, and in the Northern Hemisphere, the horns should be filled and buried between the end of September and the end of October (or March to April in the Southern Hemisphere). The use of the composted horn manure is carefully timed as well. It's first mixed with water, ideally rainwater, by stirring in one direction, then abruptly stopping the vortex, creating chaos in the water, followed by stirring in the opposite direction. This process is repeated for one hour, using this time as a sort of moving meditation, and it's best done in a pleasant, open-air location that, ideally, has been set aside for this purpose. The resulting liquid is then sprayed onto moistened soil in the evening, aiming not to drench the earth but lightly mist it, much like a homeopathic remedy that relies not on a high dosage but rather the high potency of a small, intentionally prepared dose.

Horn Silica

Another key preparation is number 501, horn silica, which makes use of quartz crystal. The crystal is finely powdered with a hammer and iron mortar, sieved to remove chunks, then mixed with water to form a smooth paste, which is packed into the cow horn. The horn should be allowed to sit until excess water rises to the top, at which point the water's poured off and the horn is topped with more quartz paste. As with 500, the silica horn is again buried, but this preparation is placed in the ground in March to April in the Northern Hemisphere (September to October in the Southern) and left for six months.

While the previous preparation, 500, is stored in a cool, dark place, the horn silica should be stored in clear jars that allow the material to catch the morning sun, emphasizing the complementary nature of these two preparations. They're also applied to the fields at different times of the year. The first is used at the beginning of the season to promote healthy root growth by enhancing microbial activity in the soil and the formation of humus, while the second is applied during the growing season to boost plant metabolism and increase resistance to disease.

All but one of the remaining preparations are used to enhance biodynamic compost, so we're going to skip ahead and take a peek at the exception, preparation 508, first, which is a tea made from horsetail (*Equisetum arvense*) or evergreen whistling pine (*Casuarina equisetifolia*). Much like the horn manures, this tea is sprayed onto the fields, in this case prior to planting, with its high silica content said to prevent fungal diseases. The tea is prepared by soaking dried horsetail in water, followed by boiling and then simmering the mixture. The tea is filtered and diluted with more water before spraying. In addition to application to bare fields, it's also said to be useful when sprayed directly onto vulnerable crops early in their growth cycle.

Biodynamic Compost

And now, on to the compost! For biodynamic compost, you first need to make preparations 502 through 507, which are yarrow, chamomile, nettle, oak bark, dandelion, and valerian. These are added to the compost pile to both enhance the composting process itself and, later, contribute to the health of the soil and plants where the compost is used.

Yarrow and Deer Bladder
Yarrow, preparation 502, is made by harvesting the flower heads when the plant is in full bloom, and the flowers, either

dried or fresh and slightly wilted (to reduce their volume) are stuffed into a dried deer bladder. Yes, you read that right: a deer bladder, which can be obtained from a biodynamic association if you don't happen to have one lying around. The bladder is soaked in lukewarm water to soften it, and then filled and tied closed with a string. The filled bladder is tied with more string on all four sides, creating a little sling from which it is hung in a sunny, open-air spot for at least three months before being buried in a pit, at the same time as horn manure 500. The bladders can be placed directly in the soil or within clay pots.

Chamomile and Cow Small Intestine

The next preparation, chamomile (503), is prepared in much the same way, but it is placed inside the small intestine of a cow, either fresh or dried. This can be hung for a few months, like the deer bladders, or buried immediately after filling. If the chamomile preparation is hung to dry, it must be moistened prior to burying it by dipping it in a bucket of water. Like the horn manure and yarrow, these are buried at the end of September to the end of October in the Northern Hemisphere and March to April in the Southern, and left for six months.

The oak bark and dandelion preparations follow this timing as well.

Stinging Nettle

Preparation 504, stinging nettle, thankfully requires no animal organs. The plants are harvested using protective gloves and used either fresh (wilted) or dried. If using dried leaves, moisten them with a lukewarm tea made from nettle leaves before burying. The container can be a wooden crate, a basket, or a clay pot or tube, and the leaves are stuffed tightly to fill the container firmly and evenly. Take care to separate the nettles from the surrounding soil, either by placing a stone or tile over the pot opening before burying or wrapping the basket or crate in sackcloth. Unlike the other preparations, nettle is left in the ground for an entire year.

Oak Bark and Livestock Skull

Next is oak bark, preparation 505, made by collecting bark from either a living oak tree (any *Quercus* species can be used), taking care not to remove too much and causing damage to the tree, or from branches sawn from an older tree. In either case, the bark must first be thoroughly cleaned of lichen and moss with a wire brush before being finely crushed, moistened, and stuffed inside—ready yourself—the brain cavity of the skull of a livestock animal, such as a cow, horse, or goat. The skulls are placed in a wooden or plastic barrel, which is filled with partially rotten, muddy plant material and soil. Water should be allowed to occasionally flow through the barrel as it sits for six months, perhaps by placing the barrel where rainwater will course through the mixture, exiting through an outspout or hole near the bottom.

Dandelion and Cow Omentum or Mesentary

Preparation 506 is made from dandelion flowers, which must be harvested when the center of the flower is still closed and only the outer petals have unfurled. The dried or wilted fresh flowers are stuffed inside an animal sheath, made from either the omentum of a cow with the fatty portions removed or the mesentery. The plants are wrapped in the material, and if being hung for three months, tied carefully with string and placed in a sunny, open-air spot, or they can be buried immediately (dip in water before burying), either directly in the soil or within earthenware containers.

Valerian

And finally, preparation 507, valerian, which is delightfully simple in comparison to the previous mixtures. Harvest the open flowers with as little stem as possible (or remove the stems later), then grind the fresh flowers into a pulp using a mortar and pestle. Fill a clean glass container with the pulp and water in a ratio of one part pulp to two parts water, filling the jar completely to reduce the presence of air, which can foster the growth of microorganisms. Dried flowers can also be used by grinding them into a powder and using a ratio of one part powder to ten parts water.

The jar should be placed in a bright location out of direct sunlight and carefully stirred each day at sunrise and sunset for three and a half days. Then, the mixture is strained into a clean jar and swirled at sunrise and sunset for the next three and a half days. Finally, the mixture is decanted into a brown glass bottle and stored in a cool, dry place. (Okay, maybe calling this process "simple" is a tad misleading, but at least there's a decided absence of deer bladders.) As fermentation can occur for the first few weeks, the bottles shouldn't be tightly sealed during this period to allow gases an escape route.

Completing the Compost Pile

And now, the moment you've been waiting for: using the preparations with compost! With a sharpened wooden stick, bore holes in your compost pile, spaced at regular intervals. One preparation will be used per hole. Take roughly a teaspoon of preparation in your hand and surround it with soil or compost to form a little ball, dropping it into one of the holes. Fill the rest of the hole with soil or compost, and use this process for preparations 502 through 506. For the valerian preparation (507), stir five milliliters of the liquid into three to five liters of lukewarm water, stirring for ten to fifteen minutes. Then, you can either pour this liquid into a hole of its own, or disperse it over the top of the entire compost pile.

Finally, cover the pile with grass, straw, leaves, and the like. To turn or not to turn the compost pile is a matter of opinion (and much debate). If you choose to turn it, this can be done after four to six weeks, at which time you can also apply another round of preparations and additional water if the pile seems excessively dry. The compost can also be left unturned, and while it can take the material longer to decompose, leaving it intact might be more likely to leave organic networks within the pile, particularly fungal, intact.

Congratulations, you have successfully made a biodynamic compost pile!

Resources

Bucher, Anne, and Rolf Bucher. *Biodynamic Preparations Manual.* Darmstadt, Germany: Biodynamic Federation, 2020. https://www.biodynamics.com/preparations.

Masson, Pierre. *A Biodynamic Manual: Practical Instructions for Farmers and Gardeners.* Edinburgh, UK: Floris, 2014.

Steiner, Rudolf. (1993). *Agriculture: Spiritual Foundations for the Renewal of Agriculture.* Junction City, OR: Bio-Dynamic Farming and Gardening Association, 1993.

Cooking

Pies

≫ Dawn Ritchie ≪

For some time now, I've earned the reputation as the pie maker in the family. When asked to bring a dish for holiday events, the request is inevitably pie. I've always loved baking. Before I became a professional writer, I even endured a brief stint as an apprentice pastry chef in a couple of celebrity chefs' kitchen. But my real teacher was my late grandmother, who made the very best cherry pie in the world. I once asked her the secret to her perfect crust. Because in the end, pastry is everything. She looked me dead in the eyes and said simply, "Lard."

Pie: The Culinary Trifecta

Pies are complex. Savory or sweet, they can perform as hors d'oeuvres, entrées, or dessert. But unless you have a baker in the family, pies tend to be reserved for holiday tables. The reason is pies take time. The pastry needs to rest in the fridge and fillings made from scratch must macerate in their own juices. A pie is not at all like a cake mix, blended in ten minutes and frosted with a can of store-bought frosting. A pie is a labor of love. And it is experienced precisely the same way. Savored, bite by bite, as pastry and filling swirl over your taste buds in a conversation between ingredients.

Want to win the night at a potluck dinner? Bring a home-baked pie. You're sure to be the one leaving the event with an empty dish.

The Importance of Pastry

Historically, the pastry crust for a pie was used only as a container for the filling. It was tough and flavorless and not particularly edible. Over the centuries, bakers developed more edible crusts. Today there are crunchy sweet crusts, buttery, flaky pastries, and crumb crusts. You can even add herbs and the zest of fruits to a crust for added excitement. Choosing the right pastry for the right pie and making it your own is part of the adventure.

Pastry Crust: For Standard Fruit or Cream Pies
2⅓ cups all-purpose flour

½ teaspoon salt

¼ cup chilled butter

½ cup chilled lard

5 tablespoons ice water

Squirt of lemon juice or tiny splash of vinegar

Combine all dry ingredients. Mix the fat into the flour until crumbly, then add the ice water and lemon juice (or vinegar). Bring the mixture together into a ball but work the pastry as little as possible. The more you work it, the tougher and less flaky it will be. Depending on the grind of your flour, you may need to increase your butter content slightly to bring the dough together. Do not increase the water.

Chill the dough ball for 15 minutes, then bring it back out and roll it out into a pie shape about ¼ inch thick. Roll from the center outward, working each section as minimally as possible. You want to shape the dough, not massage it back and forth. Light and flaky, not tough and rubbery, is your goal.

Sweet Short Crust: Useful for Tarts

1½ cup cake or pastry flour

½ cup powdered confectioner's sugar

¼ teaspoon salt

½ cup cold butter

1 egg yolk

This is a sweet pastry with a cookie-like texture. Make it in a food processor. Mix the dry ingredients. Cube the butter into mixture. Pulse to incorporate. Add the yolk. Pulse until it comes together. Chill the dough ball in fridge. Roll out and press into the tart pan.

Hot Water Crust: Firm, Forgiving, and Hearty Enough for Savory Fillings

This old-fashioned British-style pastry is used frequently for game or pork pies. It's not the yummiest crust in the world, but it serves the purpose of holding the filling intact for a serious bake. It's often used with a springform pan or the classic old-fashioned oval game molds that produce showstoppers for a buffet spread.

2¼ cup all-purpose flour

2 teaspoons salt

1¼ cup water

½ cup lard

Combine dry ingredients in a bowl. Bring the water to a boil and add the lard to the pot. Make a well in the center of the flour mixture. Slowly add the hot water and lard solution to the flour. Mix to a ball. Knead briefly. Cover and refrigerate for 20 minutes. Roll dough on a lightly floured surface to ¼ inch thick.

Cornmeal Crust: Perfect for a Savory Galette or a Pot Pie

¾ cup cornmeal

1¾ cup all-purpose flour

1 teaspoon salt

½ teaspoon sugar

1 cup cold butter, cubed

6 tablespoons ice water

Mix dry ingredients. Cut in pea-size pieces of butter. Mix quickly with fingers till crumbly. Add water. Refrigerate dough ball for 5 minutes before using. Roll thin. It is very buttery and will puff up.

Streusel: An Inviting Sweet Topping in Lieu of a Top Crust

½ cup dark brown sugar, packed in firmly

¾ cup all-purpose flour

½ teaspoon salt

1 teaspoon cinnamon

¼ cup ground almonds (or almond flour; if you don't have almond flour, increase all-purpose flour to 1 cup)

6 tablespoons chilled unsalted butter

Combine all dry ingredients, mix together, then work in the cold butter with a pastry cutter, a fork, or your fingers to a coarse texture. Streusel goes on top of the filling before it goes into the oven.

Prebaking a Bottom Crust

Some recipes call for a prebaked bottom crust to prevent soggy bottoms. Roll out your pastry shell, lay it inside your pie plate, and then chill as you preheat your oven to 350°F. After the oven is preheated, line the shell with parchment paper and add pie weights to keep the pastry from heaving while baking. Pop in the oven for 25 minutes.

Tools of the Trade

Rolling Pins

Rolling pins are a must-have and come in various materials. There's the classic wooden rolling pin, stainless-steel, marble, or plastic. I prefer wood, because that's what I started with. Give it a light dusting of flour before use to prevent fat globules from sticking to the roller.

Pie Plates

Pie plates are either deep dish or standard size and are ceramic, aluminum disposables, or the standard oven-proof glass variety. Glass is my go-to for zero waste and lends the ability to check the bottom of the crust to ensure it is fully baked.

Tart Pans and Molds

Tart pans also come in various configurations, from ceramic and glass to metal. A metal nonstick tart pan with a fluted edge and a removable bottom will serve you well for anything from quiche to a lemon tart. Springform pans and game or pâté molds hold a deep-dish entrée and permit quick release for plating up.

Pie Weights

A nice addition to your culinary toolbox is ceramic pie weights. Use them to prevent the crust from heaving when you pre-bake a crust. A container of reusable pie weights go for under ten dollars. A cheaper version is a simple bag of dried beans that can be bought for a buck, which I use over and over.

Crust Shield

The first thing that burns on your pie is the outer edge of the crust. Solution: a ring of metal with a big hole in the center that rims the outer edges of your crust. If you don't own one, you can always fashion a makeshift ring from aluminum foil.

Pastry Cutter

A handle with five or six circular stainless steel wires attached will allow you to blend cold fats into your pastry flour without warming them with your hands.

Let's Bake Some Pies

A Salute to Sour: Rhubarb Pie

Rhubarb is one of the early party guests to the veggie patch each spring (we consider it a fruit, but it's really a vegetable), and what better purpose for this tangy vegetable than a pie?

When harvesting, don't take it all at once. Harvest only a third from each plant, and it will continue to produce. Twist the stalk gently near the base until it releases and cracks off. Then give it a gentle yank. Remove the leaves and compost them. They are not edible.

Clean, dry, and chop the stalks into little cubes, ¼ to ½ inch. Use right away or freeze in a freezer bag so you can enjoy pie, compote, or jam throughout the year. Rhubarb freezes well. If you have an abundance, don't let it wither and die.

The Filling

I'm a bit of a purist when it comes to rhubarb pie. I don't believe it needs a custard base to swim in, nor the addition of strawberries to make it palatable. I like to experience the tartness and texture of the rhubarb in all its glory, adding only enough sugar to mitigate that slightly sour hit on your taste buds.

Our taste buds are designed to experience sweet, salty, bitter, sour, and umami. By embracing a bit of tanginess, we hone our palette, opening ourselves to new culinary experiences. So, allow a little astringent in, instead of smothering everything you eat in sugar or salt.

Experiment with the recipe that follows and adjust how much sugar you will add in your rhubarb filling. If you have a sweet tooth, start with the full recipe and use the streusel topping. Reduce the amount of sugar over time to experience more of the sour flavor that will fill out your tongue's potential.

9 cups chopped rhubarb, washed, dried thoroughly, and cut into ½-inch lengths

½ to ¾ cup sugar

½ cup honey

4 tablespoons tapioca

¼ teaspoon salt

Light squeeze of lemon

Rhubarb pie can be topped either with a full pastry crust, a lattice crust, or a streusel topping. If you went light on the sweetener in the filling, streusel will bring the sweet and moderate the tanginess nicely. For a savory flavor use a pastry top crust.

Preparation

Combine all filling ingredients in a bowl and let it macerate while you prepare your pastry. Use the pie pastry recipe for your bottom crust and prebake it.

Prebake

Put the pastry in the pie plate, line it with parchment, add pie weights, and bake the crust in a 350°F oven for 25 minutes. When the timer goes off, remove the parchment and pie weights. Don't burn yourself on the hot pie plate. Pour the filling into the warm crust and top it with either an upper crust or a streusel topping.

This pie really works with the streusel topping, but if you use pastry for a top crust, jab a couple of slices in the crust to vent and brush it with whipped egg wash. Wrap aluminum foil around the edges of the pastry so it won't burn.

Place in the oven to bake for 1 hour and 20 minutes or until the juices run and bubble up.

For the Sweet Tooth: Forage Frangipane Tart

Frangipane is a traditional crème pâtissière with the addition of ground almonds. Like most pastry creams, it is composed primarily of creamed butter, eggs, sugar, cream, and a dash of flour. The texture you'll ultimately end up with will have much to do with how finely you grind your almonds.

The frangipane cream base sits inside a short crust. From the bottom up you'll have three layers: the short crust, the frangipane, then your fruit topping. As it bakes, the frangipane will puff up and envelop your fruit, so don't overcrowd your fruit topping. Leave room for that rise.

I offer several choices in this recipe, because as a baker, experimenting and turning a dessert into your signature dish is the mark of a trailblazer, and that's what Forage Frangipane is all about. Let the adventure begin with a wilderness hike foraging for your fruit topping, be it wild berries from a bramble, cherries, figs, plums, pears, or an apple-picking trip to an orchard. It's truly thrilling coming home with a basket of foraged goods. It's like hitting the wilderness lottery and the eating is sublime, teeming with vitamins and nutrients.

Poaching Fruits

If you are using hard fruits like apples or pears, poach first in a simple syrup (2:1 sugar to water) for 10 minutes to soften. Let cool before slicing. For softer fruits like peaches or berries, just slice and glaze lightly with a sugar syrup, jam, or jelly. I made a frangipane, for example, with sliced nectarines and cherry preserves and used the cherry syrup as a glaze.

Frangipane Filling

   1½ cup almonds (to make ¾ cup finely ground)

   ½ cup soft unsalted butter

   ½ cup sugar

   1 tablespoon cake and pastry flour

1 egg

Finely grated zest of a lemon or an orange

¼ cup heavy whipping cream

1 teaspoon pure vanilla extract

2 tablespoons rum (Replace with any liqueur that enhances your choice of fruit. If you use cherries, you might want to use Kirsch instead.)

About 1½ cups fruit topping of your choice

Filling Preparation

Ensure all ingredients are at room temperature before proceeding.

Using a food processor, grind approximately 1½ cup almonds to a fine powdery texture. You want to end up with ¾ cup ground almonds. Keep an eye on the grind so you don't create almond paste or butter.

Cream the soft butter and sugar in a mixer. Add the flour.

Add the egg and blend well. Add the zest. Add the heavy cream. Mix in your flavorings (vanilla and liqueur). Your pastry cream should be light and fluffy before you fold in your almonds. Fold in ground almonds.

Preheat oven to 350°F.

Prepare a Short Crust

Use the short crust recipe, press it into an 8-inch tart pan with a removable bottom, and smooth the frangipane in. Top it with the sliced fruit of your choice. Be sure to leave a bit of space around the fruit for the frangipane to swell up.

Bake in a 350°F oven for 50 minutes.

This pie is very rich and sweet, yet subtle in flavor. For the sophisticated diner who enjoys a smaller slice with their espresso.

Luscious Umami: Wild Mushroom Galette

When I mention a mushroom pie to people, their faces scrunch up, their brows furrow, and they are not shy about their reservations. Won't it be watery? Slimy? The color will look awful, and so on. But a cornmeal crust and a rustic wild mushroom galette packed with oniony ramps, greens, herbs, and a creamy dose of either goat's cheese or ricotta can deliver a satisfying dose of umami to a buffet table.

A galette is basically a pie made without a pie plate. Roll out a crust, lay in the filling, and then fold the edges inward and crimp, sealing it with egg wash. Some of the filling should peek out of the raggedy crust, and each galette can be individually-sized—a wonderful appetizer to warm up guests as they arrive.

If you can't find fresh wild mushrooms, buy dried varieties and rehydrate with a little water, ensuring to press the liquid out as much as possible before adding them to the pie filling. Porcini are a good option, as are shitake, chicken of the woods, black trompettes, and cremini. Mushrooms have awesome antioxidant properties, so they are a great addition to our daily diets.

If you don't have ricotta cheese on hand, heat a pot of milk until it steams. Do not boil. Remove from heat, add a tablespoon of vinegar (or lemon juice), and you will see it separate into curds. Add more vinegar or lemon if needed. Strain off the whey liquid and salt to taste. Instant ricotta.

Filling

    3 cups sliced wild mushrooms

    1 tablespoon olive oil

    2 tablespoons unsalted butter

    1½ cups leeks or ramps (wild leeks if you can find them)

    2 cloves garlic (mash to a paste in a mortar and pestle)

    2 tablespoons cooking wine

    ½ teaspoon thyme

    ½ teaspoon parsley

    ½ teaspoon salt

    2 cups chopped greens of your choice (spinach, beet greens, Swiss chard, etc.)

    1 cup chèvre (goat's cheese) or ricotta

    1 beaten egg (use as egg wash for pastry)

    Finely chopped Italian parsley or chives to garnish

Preparation

Prepare the cornmeal pastry for this dish. Preheat oven to 400°F.

Lightly sauté mushrooms in the oil and butter. Remove to a plate.

Sauté the leeks (or ramps) until they become translucent. Add in garlic. Add in cooking wine, herbs, and salt (cooking wine has salt in it so do not over salt). Add in greens and cook until just wilted. Return mushrooms to pan and heat through.

Roll out dough into 6–8 sections (small pancake sizes). Spread a thin layer of goat cheese or ricotta on the dough. Layer in the mushrooms and greens. Fold the dough edges in, leaving some mushroom exposed. Brush dough with egg wash.

Place on a baking pan lined with parchment paper. Bake at 400°F for 30–35 minutes. Garnish lightly with chopped parsley or chives. Serve warm. Serves 6–8.

Don't throw out the whey from your ricotta.
Save it to cook rice or add to a soup or stew.

Holiday Harvest: Pumpkin Pie

Thanksgiving happily arrives right during the pumpkin harvest. Making a pumpkin pie from scratch is far easier than most know and the taste is superior to canned pumpkin. You also get the joy of visiting a pumpkin patch or plucking one from your own garden. Sugar pumpkins are small. You don't want a big ole jack-o'-lantern.

Preparation

First, bake your pumpkin and carve out the soft, cooked mash. Preheat the oven to 375°F, line a baking sheet with aluminum foil, and slice the sugar pumpkin in half. Remove the seeds and fibrous interior and remove the stem. Rub the skin with a tiny bit of vegetable oil.

Place each half face down on the baking sheet in a 375°F oven for 1 hour. Check at around 45 minutes with a fork. The fork should go through easily. Let cool.

Carve out the soft pulp and mash it up. Discard the outer shell in your compost bin.

Filling

> 2 cups cooked pumpkin puree
>
> ½ cup whole milk
>
> 1 cup heavy whipping cream
>
> ½ cup granulated sugar
>
> ½ cup dark brown sugar
>
> 2 eggs
>
> 1 teaspoon ginger
>
> 1 teaspoon ground cinnamon
>
> ½ teaspoon freshly ground nutmeg
>
> ¼ teaspoon allspice
>
> ½ teaspoon salt
>
> ⅛ teaspoon pepper
>
> 1 tablespoon bourbon (optional)
>
> Beaten egg (egg wash for pastry crust decorations)

Combine all ingredients and let stand at room temperature while you prepare a standard pastry crust. The batter should resemble pancake batter. Add more cream to thin as necessary.

Preheat the oven to 350°F and prebake the bottom crust for 10 minutes (you are just warming the bottom crust, not doing a full prebake).

Raise the oven temperature to 400°F. Pour the filling into warm crust. No top crust is used for a pumpkin pie. Use any leftover pastry to make decorative leaves for the edges of the pie. Brush the pastry with egg wash.

Bake in a 400°F oven for 35–40 minutes or until the center still looks slightly jiggly. It will firm up once out of the oven. Cool to fully set. Serve with bourbon-flavored whipped cream.

Green Tea

≈ Suzanne Ress ≈

I'd heard and read about the purported health benefits of green tea for years: it is a significant source of antioxidants and polyphenols, which are said to protect against breast, prostate, and colorectal cancers; it lowers the possibility of heart disease by helping to improve cholesterol levels; and it contains epigallocatechin-3-gallate, which possibly protects against Alzheimer's and Parkinson's diseases. Green tea contains both caffeine and theanine, which work together to keep a person alert but calm.

I had tried green tea a number of times, but as I was more of a coffee drinker, green tea was just another

beverage I might drink a few times a year, without giving it much thought.

Then, while on vacation sightseeing with friends in Colorado, we stopped into an independently run coffee shop for an afternoon pick-me-up. My previous experience with coffee shops was limited to emergencies: for example, while travelling, if I got up earlier than the hotel breakfast was being served and there was no in-room coffee maker. But that afternoon, not wanting to drink coffee but desiring something cool and refreshing, I ordered an iced matcha latte, unsweetened, made with whole cow's milk. Served in a tall, biodegradable cup, it was immensely satisfying—naturally sweet because of the milk and the good-quality matcha, cool, refreshing, and invigorating.

A week later, while waiting for a flight, I decided to buy an iced matcha latte at the airport chain coffee shop, and was very disappointed. I could hardly taste the matcha, and the drink was loaded with sugar and crushed ice. I realized that the way in which matcha is made and served makes a big difference in its flavor.

Looking further into the subject, I found that there are various grades of matcha, and a lot of variation in quality and taste depending on the grade. I also began to realize that what is called "green tea" is not only the pretty green matcha, but a whole dimension of very diverse teas, and most of them do not look green when brewed!

What Is Green Tea?

Green teas originated in China two thousand years ago. All real teas, called *cha* in Chinese, Japanese, and Korean, are made from the *Camellia sinensis* plant, a relative of flowering evergreen camellia shrubs and small trees in gardens and parks.

Camellia sinensis is native to southeast Asia. The difference between green tea and other kinds of tea is how the leaves are prepared after picking. Green tea leaves are prepared by picking the fresh green leaves, then letting them wither very briefly or sometimes not at all, then cooking them, either by steam or hot plate. Then they are pressed or rolled to remove excess moisture and dried in hot air or on a hot pan. Because the leaves are left to wither only very briefly, green teas preserve more of the qualities of the fresh tea leaf, such as phenolic compounds, astringency, and vegetal flavors, than other kinds of tea.

Leaves for non-green teas are allowed to wither for much longer periods of time and may be pressed or rolled repeatedly. This changes their flavor and the chemical compounds in the leaves.

Green teas are called *green* because the leaves used to make it are green, but in most cases the actual brewed tea is golden, yellowish-green, or even red-brown in color, with the exception of matcha. Matcha is finely powdered high-quality green tea leaves that are beat into the liquid, rather than being infused like most other teas.

Is yerba maté a green tea? Sort of, yes, although because it is not made from the *Camellia sinensis* plant, it should not be called "tea" at all. It is made instead from the leaves of a variety of *Ilex*, an evergreen shrub in the holly family, which is native to South America. A yerba maté beverage is made by infusing the plant's dried leaves and twigs in hot or cold water. Its flavor is vegetal and grassy, similar to some types of green tea. Yerba maté is also high in flavonoids, antioxidants, polyphenols, and minerals and contains caffeine. Unlike tea (cha), it does not contain theanine.

Most green teas go by their Chinese or Japanese names. In Japanese, *matcha* means "fine-powdered cha"; *sencha* means "steeped cha"; *bancha* is "common cha"; and *genmaicha* is "roasted rice cha," for example. Two exceptions that come to mind are white tea (*hakugouginshin* in Japanese and *bai cha* in Chinese), which is really a green tea, and gunpowder green tea. Gunpowder green tea was introduced to English people in Taiwan in the 1800s, and its pellet-shaped leaves reminded them of gunpowder, although the original Chinese name, *zhu cha*, means "pearl tea," because to the Chinese the pellets looked like little pearls.

Brewing Green Tea

I'd always believed that tea should be brewed in boiling hot water, the British way, but, in fact, green teas are meant to be brewed in water below boiling temperature, so while water boils at 100 degrees Celsius (212 degrees Fahrenheit), green tea should be brewed between 70 and 80 degrees Celsius (158 to 176 degrees Fahrenheit) and can even be brewed in cool water! Cooler than boiling water temperature and short infusion times (one to three minutes, in most cases) make for a lighter, non-bitter tea. Experiment with water temperatures and brewing times, as both have an impact on the taste of the tea.

Japanese Green Teas

Generally, Japanese green teas taste more vegetal and bitter than Chinese green teas, due to the difference in the way the tea leaves are processed. There are many, many types of green tea, but I will cover some of the most popular.

Sencha means "infused or steeped tea," and it includes many subvarieties and various grades and qualities. *Sincha* ("first tea") is highly prized, made from tender young leaves picked in early April before the rains come and the camellia plants start their fast growth period. It is difficult to obtain and is considered to be the best of all senchas. I was able to try *sencha kaori*, which my tea advisor said was similar to *sincha*, and was blown away by the wonderful hay-like, almost spinachy, green corn smell of the leaves and sweet taste of the tea.

Kabusecha is another type of sencha, and it is grown in the shade to increase the leaves' amino acids, such as theanine, which changes the tea's flavor and makes it more invigorating.

Genmaicha is green tea with hulled, boiled, roasted brown rice added to extend the tea. It was originally considered a poor peoples' tea but has become popular with everyone because of its unusual smoky, nutty, mellow flavor.

Kukicha ("stem tea") is another "inferior" green tea, made from the roasted tea stems. It too has a mellow, roasted, lovely toasty flavor, and is golden red-brown when brewed.

Hojicha is another roasted tea, although this one is carefully roasted in a porcelain pot over high heat, which turns the leaves reddish-brown. It has an earthy aroma and a pleasing smoky taste and is lower in caffeine than some of the other green teas, so is a good one to drink throughout the day.

Tamaryokucha ("coiled tea"), also known as *guricha* ("curled tea"), has leaves that are rolled into little comma-like shapes. It has a mild, fruity, slightly tangy, and less-astringent taste.

Bancha ("common tea") is made from mature leaves that are left over throughout the picking season, and is considered inferior in flavor. It contains less caffeine, less flavonoids, less plant alkaloids, and less flavor than sencha teas or matcha.

Matcha, well-known nowadays, is also the greenest looking. It is made by finely grinding the dried green leaves of *tencha*, which is considered one of the highest grades of green tea leaves, grown in the shade for a few weeks before harvesting to increase theanine and caffeine content. Matcha comes in many grades, which are reflected by the price. The finest, tea-ceremony grade matcha is quite costly and is sold in small quantities with special wrappings, while lower-quality matcha is much cheaper but should be used mainly for cooking. A matcha beverage is prepared using a special bamboo whisk, and the ground tea leaves are whisked briskly into warmed water (could also be milk, if you are making a latte) until it becomes frothy.

Chinese Green Teas

Green tea first originated in China and was then brought into Japan and Korea. Chinese green teas have a very different taste from Japanese, as the way the leaves are treated after picking is different. Chinese green teas are pan roasted after picking rather than being steamed, and this results in, generally, a less astringent flavor.

Long Jing ("dragon well") is an ancient, high quality, imperial green tea that originated in Long Jing village. Its leaves are chopped and pressed, but in much larger pieces than most Japanese green teas. The leaves have a fantastic fresh, green, hay-like odor even while dry, and once they are steeped, this aroma becomes intoxicating. The steeped leaves can be eaten! The flavor of the tea is mild, sweet, and rounded, and this tea is supposed to be especially high in cholesterol-reducing catechins.

The white tea *yin zhen* ("silver needle") was first made in China about four hundred years ago. Japan has its own form of white tea, mentioned earlier, *hakugouginshin*. All white teas are made from the soft white down-covered buds of the tea plant, wilted briefly and sometimes steamed or cooked. White tea's flavor is delicate and mild, refreshing, especially cold. It has even higher antioxidant properties than other green teas, with the associated health benefits.

Huang shan mao fung ("yellow mountain fur petal") is produced in the Anhui province of China. The leaves have a needle-like form and a clean, floral scent. The tea is considered a "China famous tea" and has an elegant, flowery taste.

Other well-known Chinese green teas are *chun mee,* which is supposed to have a slightly acidic, plumlike flavor; *biluochun,* with leaves curled like snails, has a fruity, delicate taste; and *Lu'an melon seed,* also grown in the Anhui province, is said to have a grassy taste and contains no melon seeds!

Korean Green Teas

Korea also has a long tradition of tea production and consumption, although, for various reasons, it is more difficult to find Korean green tea, *nokcha,* in non-Korean markets. Korean green teas are named according to when they are picked, the first picked, *ujeon,* is considered the highest quality. Then comes the second picked, *sejak;* the third picked, *jungjak;* and the final picking, *daejak,* which is used primarily in cooking.

Flavored Green Teas

Much of what you might find available in a non-Asian grocery store or general supermarket will likely be a form of bancha green tea with floral or herbal or even seaweed additions. *Tulsi* green tea is a traditional Indian Ayurvedic remedy—green tea with tulsi, a type of basil, added. Jasmine green tea is popular and is probably the oldest flavored green tea, dating back, some say, to the fifth century, in China. If purchased loose (rather than in teabags) from a serious tea purveyor, it will probably be made of a higher quality sencha, with dried jasmine flowers added.

There is also mint green tea, chamomile green tea, honey lemon green tea, ginger lime green tea, Earl Grey green tea, and many more. Inexplicably, the type of green tea used in most commercially packaged blends is not listed, so one must assume it is probably the lowest grade. If you buy a blended green tea at a specialty tea shop, the type and quality of the green tea in the blend is usually made clear.

Flavored green teas do not taste much like green tea, usually, but more like what they've been blended with. For people who do not particularly enjoy the taste of green tea but want its health benefits, these are a good choice, and there is a wide variety to try and to choose from.

Using Green Teas in Food

Green tea can be successfully used as an ingredient in many recipes, both sweet and savory, and in cocktails, shakes, and smoothies. Try green tea in sauces for fish, vegetarian pasta, rice dishes, cookie bars, pies, puddings, and cakes.

Here are a couple of established green tea recipes I've tried and enjoyed.

Long Jing Shrimp

1 pound fresh or frozen and thawed large shrimp

2 egg whites

⅓ cup cornstarch

2 tablespoons vegetable oil

1 cup brewed Long Jing green tea and the used tea leaves

¾ cup rice wine

Toss the shrimp in the egg whites, then into the cornstarch. Fry them briefly in the vegetable oil in a pan, just 15–20 seconds, then quickly stir-fry them over high heat in a wok with hot Long Jing tea, the used tea leaves, and the rice wine until the shrimp are curled. Serve with rice. Serves 4.

Matcha Tiramisu

2 tablespoons matcha powder, plus 2 tablespoons

1 cup hot water

1 package ladyfingers (about 12)

3 eggs

4 tablespoons sugar

1 pound mascarpone

8 tablespoons powdered sugar

1 teaspoon vanilla

Mix 2 tablespoons matcha powder into the hot water and pour over the ladyfingers in a dish, then put aside. Separate the eggs. Beat the whites until stiff. Beat the yolks with 4 tablespoons sugar until light yellow. Mix together the egg yolk mixture, mascarpone, powdered sugar, vanilla, and 2 more tablespoons matcha until smooth.

Spread ¼ of this cream on the bottom of a glass dish. Place some of the soaked lady fingers over. Repeat, ending with a cream layer. Sprinkle more matcha powder over the top and refrigerate for 4 hours. Serves 4–6.

Matcha Sauce for Vegetables

    1 tablespoon matcha

    ¼ cup hot water

    3 tablespoons cornstarch

    1 cup vegetable broth

    Juice of 1 lemon

Whisk the matcha into the hot water. Mix the cornstarch into a little more water to make a smooth paste.

In a saucepan, blend broth, cornstarch mixture, lemon juice, and matcha liquid. Heat slowly, until simmering, and let simmer until it begins to thicken.

You can add crumbled nori seaweed or a little honey or other sweetening. You can substitute milk, either animal derived or vegan, for the broth. This sauce can be stored in the refrigerator and is good on steamed green beans, broccoli, zucchini, and kale, as well as on fish or tofu.

Matcha Hummus

    1 can chickpeas

    1 tablespoon tahini

    ½ cup crumbled dried nori seaweed

    Juice of ½ lemon

    1 tablespoon matcha or steeped Long Jing tea leaves

    Sesame oil

    1 tablespoon sesame seeds

    Rice crisps, to serve

Drain the chickpeas, retaining their liquid, and put them in a food processor with the tahini, nori, lemon juice, and matcha. Whiz until smooth, adding some of the chick pea liquid if necessary. Transfer to a serving bowl, drizzle on a little sesame oil, and sprinkle the sesame seeds over. Refrigerate for at least an hour before serving. Serve with rice chips.

—

Use your creativity, experiment, and try green tea in anything that strikes your fancy. You're sure to come up with a few winners! *Kampai*!

Resources

Gunnars, Kris. "10 Evidence-Based Benefits of Green Tea." Healthline.com. Last modified April 6, 2020. https://www.healthline.com/nutrition/top-10-evidence-based-health-benefits-of-green-tea#_noHeaderPrefixedContent.

Tea in Italy. 2016. https://www.teainitaly.com/.

Wildwood Potstickers

ᗌ Jordan Charbonneau ᗏ

As children, my cousin Eli and I were often given free roam of the woods around our homes and at my grandparents' cabin in the woods of Vermont. We spent hours on various imaginary quests and adventures, avoiding coming home as long as possible.

One way we were able to prolong our outdoor time was to snack on wild foods. As we plunged farther into the woods, we'd inevitably get hungry but never wanted to turn around. Plus, how could we be true adventurers if we didn't know how to live off the land?

Thankfully, we had some rudimentary knowledge of wild edibles, though I can't remember who taught

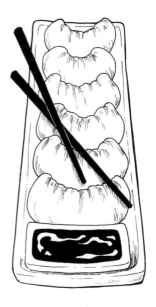

us. We ate blackberries and wood sorrel, dug Indian cucumbers (*Medeola virginiana*), and snacked on sheep sorrel, dandelion leaves, and apples from long-abandoned homesteads.

It added to the thrill. I felt wild and independent as we marched off through fields and forests, even if I was chewing apples picked so early that they were more sour than any candy or choking down bitter dandelion greens. I fell madly in love with the idea of living off the land.

As an adult, I haven't changed much. I still get excited about harvesting wild food, gardening, and spending time among the trees. Now, I'm fortunate enough to have my own spot in the Appalachian mountains surrounded by acres of forest and a husband, Scott, who shares my passion for foraging and gardening.

Spring here is one of my favorite times of the year because these hillsides are flush with edible wild greens and the gardens are waking up. On a quick walk through the woods, Scott and I can easily fill a basket with wild goodies.

These days I'm a little more knowledgeable and selective than I was all those years ago. We gather spicy ramp leaves and wild onion shoots, succulent chickweed and miner's lettuce, beautiful purple deadnettle and dogtooth violets, and one of my favorites, stinging nettle.

We're careful and slow. We leave the ramp bulbs, clipping only a few of the leaves, pinch nettles off delicately above a set of leaves, and avoid harvesting more than a third of any patch. We cultivate certain plants too. Beloved species like ramps had been completely harvested out of our property years ago, so we reintroduced them.

We also start enjoying the first harvests from the garden in the spring. We sow kale, spinach, mustards, radishes, and turnips early under row cover or in cold frames. In the spring we begin harvesting baby greens.

Using food we've grown and foraged is an amazing feeling and a privilege. I'm grateful that we're able to provide even a portion of our needs from the land that we love while caring for it too.

What Are Potstickers?

One of my favorite ways to put the spring bounty to good use is to make potstickers. With just a bit of effort, they turn simple ingredients into a savory, filling meal perfect for gathering around after a walk in the woods.

Potstickers are a type of Chinese dumpling with a crispy bottom and soft, chewy, steamed top. Who exactly invented potstickers and when is no longer known. One common and reasonable theory behind their origins is that they were created through a happy accident. They were most likely traditional steamed or boiled dumplings that were forgotten and left on too long. When all the water cooked off, they stuck to the bottom of the pan and were a hit! However they were invented, we're fortunate to have the recipe today.

Making potstickers is quite simple and is a nice recipe to have on hand for seasonal ingredients. The filling is very versatile. You can swap in a variety of homegrown or foraged herbs and vegetables depending on what's available to you at any given moment.

Dough

To make potstickers, you'll need potsticker dough or wrappers. You can find premade wrappers at some supermarkets and most Asian specialty markets. I generally prefer to make my own dough, as it's quite easy to make with just three common ingredients and is a great rainy-day activity.

For the dough, you'll need:

2½ cups all-purpose flour

1 teaspoon salt

¾ cup boiling water

To begin, set a pot of water on the stove to boil. While it's heating up, mix the flour and salt in a good-size mixing bowl. After they're mixed, make a well or depression in the center.

When the water reaches a boil, pour about half the water into the well. Begin stirring the mixture, slowly adding the rest of the water until the mixture comes together, forming clumps.

Knead the dough on a clean, lightly floured surface until it forms a smooth ball. The dough should be tacky but not sticky. Let it rest for 10–20 minutes covered with a damp cloth while you work on the filling. You can also make the dough ahead of time and store it in a container in the fridge for several days if desired.

Filling

I learned to make potstickers from a friend who stuffed them with more traditional fillings like cabbage and meat. However, I wanted to create a vegan version and incorporate foods that were frequently available on our homestead. I love the way different combinations of greens and root vegetables keep the recipe from getting boring through the seasons. The milder vegetables also do a great job soaking up some of the stronger seasonings like garlic, soy sauce, red pepper, and ginger.

For the filling, you'll need:

½ cup uncooked rice

1½ tablespoons freshly grated ginger

1 medium-size carrot, shredded (turnips or beets would also work well)

1 cup chopped greens (nettles, chickweed, kale, spinach, etc.)

1 handful diced onions, ramp leaves, wild onions, or a combination of these

2–3 cloves garlic, minced

3 tablespoon soy sauce

1 teaspoon red pepper flakes (optional)

Cook your rice according to the package instructions. While it's cooking, combine the ginger, carrots, greens, onions, and garlic in a large mixing bowl.

When the rice is done, add it to the mixing bowl. Stir in the soy sauce and red pepper flakes.

If you've got other vegetables on hand, you can swap in your own additions. We've tried cabbage, finely diced peppers, sprouts, and shredded cauliflower. Just be sure you dice or shred your vegetables finely so that they're easy to fold into wrappers and cook quickly and evenly. Also, be aware that really juicy vegetables like tomatoes could make your potstickers soggy.

Dipping Sauce

You can prepare the dipping sauce fresh or make it ahead of time and store it in the fridge. I love creating a sweet and salty combination with soy sauce and maple syrup. If maple syrup isn't available to you, you can always try a pinch of sugar instead. If you want to avoid sugar altogether, 1–2 tablespoons of apple cider vinegar is a great addition.

For the sauce, you'll need:

2 tablespoons maple syrup

8 tablespoons soy sauce

2 teaspoons grated ginger

4 cloves garlic, minced

1 teaspoon of red pepper flakes

Combine all the ingredients. Serve in individual dishes for dipping potstickers.

Putting It All Together

To make the potstickers, roll out some of your dough on a lightly floured surface. You want to roll it out as thin as possible.

Using a glass, mug, or biscuit cutter, cut out circles. Place a spoonful of filling into each potsticker. Moisten the edges of the wrapper with a bit of water on your finger. You may be able to skip this step with fresh dough.

Fold the wrapper over the dough, creating a half circle. Pinch or pleat the edge together, basically creating little folds along the open edge.

Heat a frying pan over medium-high heat with a thin layer of oil, about 1–2 tablespoons, in the bottom of the pan. We usually use olive oil, but other vegetable oils work too.

Make sure you select a pan with a lid that fits well. You'll need it to steam the tops. I love my cast-iron skillet for this.

When the oil is hot, add your potstickers with the pleated edge up. Fry them until the bottoms are a nice golden brown. Then quickly pour about ¼ cup water into the pan and place the lid on so that it fills with steam. Cook for 10–15 minutes, until most of the water is gone and the tops are a bit translucent.

Garnish with some extra diced ramp or wild onions and serve hot with dipping sauce. Don't be surprised if they're gone quickly. It's easy to stuff yourself on just these. They also make a great, unique appetizer for gatherings or an excellent side for Asian-inspired meals.

To cook additional batches, let the remainder of the water cook off, scrape any stuck-on dough out of the pan, add oil again, and then repeat the process. This recipe makes 20–25 potstickers.

Go Eat a Cactus: Edible Cacti for Medicine and Delight

꙳ Diana Rajchel ꙳

U nless you grew up with them, your first association with cacti likely involves a cartoon coyote, a roadrunner, and spikes landing in a frustrated, furry, animated keister. After seeing something like that, you might not think of eating one.

Succulent collectors and psychonauts alike can tell you "not all cacti" about the common myths. So let's introduce everyone properly: yes, cacti are succulents, but not all succulents are cacti. Agave, we're looking at you—you are most certainly *not* a cactus. The majority of the Cactaceae family retain water in thick, fleshy leaves and stems that they developed to survive dry conditions. While avid plant collectors can and do cultivate

these spiky wonders anywhere in the world, they originate almost exclusively in the Americas and the West Indies.

Perhaps because of their association with the sparse resources of the desert, only now are the medical and culinary communities homing in on what indigenous populations already know: the right cacti make good food, good building and weaving material, and good medicine.

Medical Applications

While indigenous peoples of the Americas incorporated the cacti into their lives for producing rope, cloth, food, and tonics, the world of colonized medicine is only just now gathering the data on what diseases specific cacti may treat. The most attention to date has gone to the prickly pear cactus, which shows potential for treating insulin resistance, may lower cholesterol, and has anti-inflammatory properties that may have applications in cancer treatment. Other cacti have not gained the level of attention that the prickly pear has, but curiosity about the potential of all members of the Cactaceae family is increasing.

On a practical, home-use level, without esoteric training in cactus use, your best bet to gain these benefits is to learn which cacti are edible, learn how to cook them, and then enjoy them. Bear in mind that relatively few cacti are edible. Please make sure you know exactly what plant you behold before you partake.

Before You Snack: Prepare for Prickly!

Depending on the specific cactus, an intrepid cook may enjoy the leaves or the fruit. When preparing something spiky, unless you have experience handling the needles, make sure you have some garden gloves designated for kitchen use handy. Rinse the plant part you intend to use in cold water, then use a vegetable peeler or paring knife to cut away the needles right at the green bumpy part they grow from. Go over the plant two or three times and be thorough; cactus needles can irritate in much the same manner as loose fish bones.

The known edible cacti are a short list, in part because some cacti may be edible but aren't enjoyable. What follows here is a non-exhaustive list; also, what we like is neurologically wired—you just might enjoy what someone else thinks of as "not so tasty."

Nopales, or Prickly Pear (*Opuntia*)

Stacks of the flat-paddled leaves from the prickly pear cactus are a familiar sight at California farmer's markets. Often, only chefs buy these paddles because of the daunting obstacle presented by the needles. Some *mercados* have mercy on us and sell the leaves sliced and pre-cut.

There are compelling reasons to brave the needles: medical research points to nopales lowering cholesterol and balancing blood sugar. You can grab these benefits just by throwing chopped leaves into your breakfast smoothie, or if you want something a little more foodie-inclined, try the vegan-adaptable recipe that follows.

The more popular part of nopales is its fruit, the prickly pear. The fruit also has needles, and they do have to be removed before consumption. The fruit has a sweet flavor that borders on syrupy, depending on its ripeness. After removing the spiky bits, enjoy the fruit raw or add it to fruit-based dishes, sauces, or beverages.

Nopales-Stuffed Avocados

1 cup chopped nopales

1 tablespoon olive oil

1 teaspoon salt

1 teaspoon minced garlic

1 ripe avocado

1 teaspoon lime juice

Feta cheese to taste (optional)

Fry the nopales in olive oil over high heat, adding salt. Reduce the heat to medium, place a lid over the pot, and cook for 20 minutes, allowing the gel the plant secretes to dry. After 15 minutes of cooking, add the garlic and stir in thoroughly. If, at the end of 20 minutes the gel has not dried, cook for about 5–7 minutes longer, adding oil and garlic as needed.

Slice the avocado in half, remove the pit, and set the halves on a plate. Sprinkle lime juice over it to slow oxidation. Spoon the nopales mixture into the avocado, and garnish with feta cheese if desired.

This dish pairs well with tilapia tacos and red cabbage.

Pitaya, or Dragon Fruit Cactus
(*Hylocereus undatus*)

The white-fleshed pitaya often inhabits the "exotic" fruit section of American grocery stores; it looks like a red alien with a green goatee that landed next to the papayas and guavas. All we know about where the pitaya originated is that it was somewhere in the Americas. Despite this, people in Asian cultures consume far more dragon fruit than the rest of the world. This cactus is unusual in that it grows as a vine and spreads over rocks and trees. The fruit is high in fiber, magnesium, and iron, making it wonderfully refreshing.

It takes relatively little effort to prepare dragon fruit for eating. All you need to do is slice it in half and dig in with a spoon. The red flesh on the outside makes a useful serving container. Some people slice the fruit, place it in their freezer for one hour, and then enjoy it like they might a sorbet.

Saguaro Cactus (*Carnegiea gigantea*)

The saguaro cactus grows in the Sonoran Desert. It has so many uses that its roots extend into the cosmologies of indigenous peoples in Arizona. The Hohokam tribe used the dead cacti as water canteens and building material. The Tohono O'odham told of the saguaro once being a human being, an aspect still honored by the tribe. As part of that tradition, they make a ritual beverage from it that honors the summer rains. The Pima used the fruit also as a medicine that helped stimulate milk flow after childbirth.

In non-traditional use, saguaro fruit is used as a smoothie additive or as an addition to dessert sauces. This simple jam recipe, while a little time-consuming, can give you some delectable ways to enjoy the fruit.

Saguaro Fruit Jam

    4 cups saguaro fruit pulp

    Water

    2 cups agave syrup (optional)

Place the saguaro fruit pulp in a pot and add water to cover. Soak for 90 minutes. Cook for 40 minutes over low heat. Gradually strain out the pulp and reserve. Continue to boil the liquid until a syrup remains; slowly add agave nectar if desired. Allow to cool.

Run the pulp through a strainer, removing as many seeds as possible. After seed removal, stir the pulp back into the syrup and stir until the mixture thickens and becomes textured. Store in glass jars and refrigerate immediately. Serve on toast, ice cream, or anything else that sounds good.

Broadleaf Yucca (*Yucca baccata*)

This cactus produces a red flower that bursts out of broad leaves. While perhaps not the most common of delicacies, the leaves are used to create an enzyme called rennet, used in cottage cheese production. These days, the fruit can be eaten raw, or it can be boiled, skinned, and then eaten. Enjoy sparingly, as the fruit of the yucca does have a laxative effect.

Adventurous Eating

Much of what we know about cactus consumption comes from modern practices or from historical information on how indigenous people used and consumed particular cacti. If you are looking for greater variety in your diet or want to try hyper-local cuisine, start with the cacti mentioned here. If you are not an expert in plant identification, please stick to obtaining your cacti-related foods from the grocery store or farmer's market. Some cacti can have high alkaline levels that are toxic, and certain edible and non-edible cacti species can bear a resemblance to one another.

Eating anything prickly belongs to the realm of the adventurous eaters. If you tend to be of a conservative mind about food fighting back, stick to the pitaya. For the rest, great risk—in this case, the possibility of having to pull cactus needles from your hand or tongue—can come with great culinary rewards.

Resources

Arizona Farm Bureau. "The Edible Desert." Fill Your Plate. August 12, 2015. https://fillyourplate.org/blog/the-edible-desert/.

Beckwith, Ronald. "Saguaro Fruit: A Traditional Harvest." Saguaro National Park. Resource Brief: Tucson Mountain District, January 2015.

Engols, Kimberly, and Season Eggleston. "The Incredible Edible Desert." Tucson: University of Arizona Department of Ecology and Evolutionary Biology, 2010.

Jinich, Pati. "Cactus Paddles or Nopales: Cleaning and Cooking." *Pati Jinich* (blog), June 7, 2012. https://patijinich.com/cleaning_cactus_paddles_or_nopales/.

Romanoff, Zan. "These Cacti Are Both Gorgeous and Edible." Bon Appétit. May 16, 2017. https://www.bonappetit.com/story/edible-cactus-clark-moorten.

Schnelker, Becky. "Traditional Uses of Wild Plants in the East Mountains." Bernalillo County, NM, 2011.

Shetty, Anoop A., M. K. Rana, and S. P. Preetham. "Cactus: A Medicinal Food." *Journal of Food Science Technology* 49, vol. 5 (October 2012): 530–36. doi:10.1007/s13197-011-0462-5.

"Which Types of Cacti Can You Eat?" Complete Landscaping. Accessed November 30, 2020. https://completelandscaping.com/types-cacti-can-eat/.

Buckwheat Country

🔾 Linda Raedisch 🔾

In episode six of the Korean drama *Oh My Ghost!*, Chef Kang wins the heart of his prep cook, Bong-sun, while sampling buckwheat pancakes with her. (Actually, Bong-sun's heart already belongs to him; it's Chef Kang who has to be won over.) Before I started watching K-dramas, I'd thought of buckwheat pancakes as frontier food, the kind of thing Daniel Boone might have eaten with maple syrup and a side of corn pone. In early North American cooking, buckwheat was the frontiersman's stand-in for real wheat, but in Asia, it's always had a place at the table.

Buckwheat (*Fagopyrum esculentum*) is not a grain; it's a flowering plant that yields chunky, triangular seeds. A field of buckwheat in full white or pink flower commands a certain amount of respect, but one buckwheat plant on its own looks positively weedy. If you can't tolerate gluten, you can eat buckwheat. You can also eat it on those Hindu holidays when wheat and rice are forbidden, like the nine-night Navaratri Festival that is held right after the buckwheat harvest and right before Divali in the fall. Because buckwheat matures quickly, it can be grown easily in cold climates and high altitudes where the growing season is short and the soil not particularly fertile. While it's still often considered an ersatz grain or second choice, buckwheat does occasionally get star treatment.

Just as Korea has restaurants that serve only buckwheat pancakes, the Japanese have made an art of buckwheat noodles, or *soba*. Because buckwheat contains no gluten, getting the dough to hold together during the soba-making process is a special skill, and handmade soba is considered a traditional art form. Elsewhere in Eurasia, buckwheat has a reputation as peasant fare. My German mother recalled how her grandmother used to cook a thick porridge of buckwheat

The "buck" in buckwheat comes from an old Germanic word for "beech," because the seeds, which are technically fruits, look a little like beechnuts. Beechnuts, or "mast," were the mainstay of pigs in Europe, and buckwheat, too, was often grown as food for livestock. This has contributed to its reputation as peasant fare in many parts of the world. Buckwheat was first brought to North America by the Colonists and then again by immigrants from Eastern Europe as "kasha," a porridge made of the roasted buckwheat seeds.

groats (whole seeds), spread it in a pan, and cut it into pieces when cool.

"Was it sweet?" I asked my mother.

"It must have been," she said. "Otherwise, I wouldn't have eaten it."

Buckwheat Torte

I first encountered the phenomenon of the fancy buckwheat torte in a little book called *Pharisäertorte, Teepunsch & Schwiegermutterkuchen* (*Pharisee Torte, Tea Punch & Mother-in-Law Cake*), a collection of traditional North German recipes. *Buchweizen-Preiselbeertorte* (buckwheat bilberry torte) is a specialty of the Lüneburger Heide region in Lower Saxony. Part moor, part swamp, the Lüneburg Heath is known for its purple heather, buckwheat, bilberries, and a special long-haired breed of sheep.

Rustic Buckwheat Blueberry Torte

Like the Korean buckwheat pancake, you can order buckwheat bilberry torte in a café. At its most elegant, the torte is covered entirely in whipped cream and looks a lot like the more famous Black Forest cake. My recipe leaves the sides naked, hence the "rustic" in its name. While German recipes usually call for bilberry preserves, I use frozen wild blueberries. If you're lucky enough to get fresh wild blueberries, be sure to pull out the stems.

This recipe calls for half buckwheat flour, half white flour. If you can't eat wheat, you can use all buckwheat flour, but, in that case, I recommend using Korean instead of American buckwheat flour.

For the cake:

  4 eggs

  ¾ cup sugar

  1 tablespoon hot water

  ½ teaspoon vanilla extract

  ¾ cup buckwheat flour

  ¾ cup white flour

  1 teaspoon baking powder

For the filling:

  ½ pint heavy cream

  2 tablespoons confectioner's sugar

  1 cup frozen wild blueberries, thawed

Tools and utensils:

  2 large bowls

  1 small bowl

  Electric mixer

  2 layer cake pans, greased and floured

In a large bowl, beat eggs until frothy. Add sugar, hot water, and vanilla extract and continue beating for about 10 minutes, until mixture is light yellow and thick like cream.

In the smaller bowl, combine flours and baking powder. Stir flour mixture into egg mixture. Stir until well blended but do not overstir; you don't want to make it tough.

Pour batter into pans, jiggling them so it reaches the edges. The cake will expand further in the pans. This is an Americanized recipe, but for the baking, we'll do it German style— no preheating. Put the pans in a cold oven and heat to

350°F. Bake for about 20 minutes or until cakes are springy and ever so slightly golden on top.

Cool the layers about 5 minutes and then turn onto plates or baking parchment. (The tops will glitter like mica, but, unfortunately, you're going to cover that up with the filling.)

While the layers are cooling, make the filling.

In another large bowl, beat the cream and confectioner's sugar until it's stiff enough that dollops dropped from the spoon hold their shape. Fold in the blueberries. The filling should be a nice shade of purple—like the heather on the Lüneburg Heath—with the blueberries still discernible. If the blueberries refuse to give up the ghost, so to speak, you can go at them with a potato masher.

Spread half the filling on the first layer and the other half on the top of the cake. Serves 16.

This is the perfect cake to serve with coffee on a Sunday afternoon, and the leftovers will taste even better for breakfast on Monday morning.

Buckwheat Pancakes

As for the Korean buckwheat pancakes, of course I had to try them, and since there are no Korean buckwheat pancake restaurants near me, I had to make them myself. I did not love them, and the fault may have been in the flour I used. American buckwheat flour gets its dark color and coarse texture from the brown seed coats and bits of black hull. The buckwheat flour I got at the grocery store looked like sand from the Jersey shore, which was fine for my blueberry torte but made my pancakes gritty even when combined with equal parts white flour. I had better results changing the ratio from half buckwheat flour and half white flour to one part buckwheat flour per three parts white flour, but Korean buckwheat flour, which is more refined, would be even better. I also added a quarter teaspoon of baking powder the second time around to make the pancakes a little less sticky.

The most common fillings for Korean buckwheat pancakes are scallions and napa cabbage leaves (both whole), which poke through the thin, plate-size pancakes very prettily. Most recipes tell you to lay the vegetables on top of the pancake after you have poured the batter in the pan, but my scallions came out chewy the first time, so now I add them first and pour the batter over them. You can also experiment with cilantro, nasturtiums, and other herbs from your garden, or, instead of fresh napa cabbage, add some kimchi, the salted, fermented cabbage that appears on the Korean table at every meal. If you're going to the Asian grocery store for buckwheat flour, pick up some *gochujang* (hot pepper paste) for the accompanying sauce. You can also make a sauce of sesame oil and soy sauce if you don't like spicy, or, if you're lazy like me, you can serve them with sriracha sauce straight out of the bottle.

Korean Buckwheat Pancakes

⅛ cup buckwheat flour

⅜ cup white flour

¼ teaspoon baking powder

½ teaspoon sugar

Pinch salt

½ cup water, plus 3 tablespoons

Olive oil to coat a large frying pan

2 napa cabbage leaves

2 scallions, green parts only

Mix all ingredients except the oil and vegetables. The batter should be very thin. Let sit for 10 minutes.

Heat about 1 teaspoon of oil in a large frying pan, moving the pan so the oil coats it all over. Lay half the scallion pieces in the hot pan, toward the sides. Lay 1 cabbage leaf in the middle of the pan and pour the batter over it, moving the pan so it reaches all the edges. Reduce heat and cook for 2–3 minutes, until the vegetables are slightly browned but the pancake is still pale. Flip the pancake over and press down with a spatula. Cook another 2–3 minutes. Flip out onto a plate and repeat with remaining ingredients. Serves 2.

Serve hot with the sauce (and person) of your choice. Oh, and, spoiler alert: Chef Kang and Bong-sun live happily ever after.

Resources

Hars, Silke. *Pharisäertorte, Teepunsch & Schwiegermutterkuchen: Torten und Kuchen aus der Küstenküche.* Husum, Germany: Cobra Verlag, 2013.

"Heide kocht: Buchweizentorte mit Preiselbeeren." Lüneburger Heide. August 29, 2019. Video, 17:38. lueneburger-heide.de /natur/video/17949/buchweizentorte-rezept.html. (Yes, the video is in German, but the cake-making process needs no translation, and you get to see the seventy-fourth Lüneburger Heide "Heather Queen" sitting in the background in full purple regalia, so it's worth a look.)

Lee, JinJoo. "Buckwheat Pancakes for Winter Olympics in Korea." *Kimchimari* (blog). Last modifed November 29, 2020. https:// kimchimari.com/buckwheat-pancake-korean-winter-olympics.

Marks, Copeland. *The Korean Kitchen: Classic Recipes from the Land of the Morning Calm*. San Francisco: Chronicle Books, 1999.

Rochow, Eric. "Kimcheejeon: A Korean Buckwheat Pancake Recipe." *GardenFork* (blog). Accessed December 1, 2020. gardenfork.tv /kimcheejeon-a-korean-buckwheat-pancake-recipe.

Health
and
Beauty

Real Facts about Herbal Supplements

☙ Mireille Blacke ☙

Over the last few years, the nutrition-related articles I've written for *Llewellyn's Herbal Almanac* have typically been inspired by my clients, this one being no exception. But this year's contribution also has its roots in herbal lore, rock music legend, and a pinch of nostalgia to keep things interesting.

As a registered dietitian (RD) and addiction specialist, I'm asked all types of questions, from the basic and simple (Will drinking more water really help me lose weight? *Yes.*) to the unbelievable and media-driven (Dr. X said on his show that I can eat fast food all day, not exercise, and lose fifteen pounds a week if I drink this juice! He's a doctor, so it's true, right?

No.). I encourage clients (and you) to be skeptical and question such outlandish media claims that seem misleading; instead seek evidence-based answers from reputable, unbiased, qualified experts with appropriate credentials (dietitian, pharmacist, etc.). To be clear, RDs are the nutrition experts; pharmacists are the medication/drug interaction experts.

Though weight management is the top nutrition-related reason most clients see RDs, their questions may run the gamut of topics, so RDs must be well-informed and prepared for just about anything. In fact, many of us became dietitians as a second or third career, so you'd be surprised at the (odd) knowledge and experience we might have. In my case, I spent two decades in the music business and rock radio before diving into healthcare. So when a young client's question piggybacked itself onto a healthy dose of pop culture and music history, she got a bit more than she expected.

One goal was increasing her daily non-caloric fluids, while she hated "the taste of water," and restricting her caffeine intake. In discussing herbal teas as an option, she suddenly and excitedly asked me, "Oh! Can I drink pennyroyal tea like in the song? Does it have caffeine?" She spoke so rapidly these questions became one giant super-word.

I leaned back in my chair and paused, for two reasons. First, for most of my clients, chamomile, peppermint, and lemongrass covered their herbal tea knowledge. Second, this forced collision of my past and present careers jarred me. However, the inner rocker won out. "Let me get this straight," I said, half-smiling. "'Pennyroyal Tea,' from *In Utero*," I continued, referencing the Nirvana song in question, which reveals the theme of seeking relief from intense, personal pain (gastric or emotional) via a socially acceptable, yet ultimately lethal, method of administration (poisoning oneself with tea). An unintentional message within the clever lyrics was ahead of its time: unaddressed emotional pain will find its way to the surface to express itself persistently. (Healing that pain is another topic.)

My client nodded affirmatively, smiling. I asked, "It's the *caffeine* you're worried about? Drinking pennyroyal tea will *kill* you!" Her smile widened, until she realized I wasn't joking. This client, an ardent but nascent Nirvana fan, born just a decade after their massive success circa 1992, would learn many things that day: there was life before the internet, grunge isn't new, song lyrics aren't medical advice, and herbal supplements might kill you if you think they are.

This client didn't learn about the pain that remains with me to this day, over twenty-five years after the core of Nirvana died. However, she accepted the reality of poetic license, selected several non-lethal herbal teas, and became far more careful about her food and beverage choices from then on, while I simply felt old as dirt.

. . . And inspired to write about the realities of certain herbal supplements, to inform others.

Dietary supplement usage is remarkably prevalent in the United States; the 2019 survey from the Council for Responsible Nutrition (CRN) found dietary supplement usage to be as follows in United States adults: 79 percent of those aged fifty-five and older, 81 percent of those aged thirty-five to fifty-four, and 70 percent of those aged eighteen to thirty-four. Of these, herbal (botanical) supplements are the most popular with adults aged thirty-five to fifty-four, who cite "overall health and wellness" as the reason for taking them.

Supplement Regulation

Herbal supplement usage is more accessible and measurable than ever before. (According to the CRN, the COVID-19 pandemic has not decreased supplement use thus far.) With greater use, the need for monitoring the safety, regulation, and effectiveness of these supplements similarly increases; unlike the strict regulations for prescription drugs, supplement companies aren't required to provide the United States Food and Drug Administration (FDA) with evidence of safety or effectiveness *prior to* supplements hitting your local grocery stores (or Amazon.com).

That's right: dietary (including herbal) supplements do not receive the strict evaluation, regulation, and monitoring by the FDA that prescription medications do, as supplements are considered neither food nor drugs. Herbal manufacturers must follow good manufacturing practices (GMP) to ensure that supplements are consistently processed and meet quality standards. These regulations maintain uniformity of supplement ingredients and composition, with care to remove impurities and contaminants. But FDA "approval" does not factor into the dietary/herbal supplement category as it does with prescription Herbal supplement manufacturers have a responsibility that their claims do not mislead the public, aren't false, and are supported by adequate research or evidence. However, the manufacturers aren't required to provide the FDA with the research or evidence.

There are occasions when FDA involvement is necessary. The manufacturer must report any adverse events (serious problems) related to herbal supplements to the FDA. The FDA can act against a manufacturer and distributor, including issuing warnings and removing or banning supplements from being sold when unsafe or when claims are determined to be false, misleading, or not supported by sufficient evidence.

Herbal Supplement Labeling

The FDA requires herbal supplement labels to display the supplement's name, manufacturer or distributor's name and address, serving size, amount, active ingredient, and complete list of ingredients (located in the Supplement Facts Panel or under it). However, the herbal supplement label doesn't require FDA approval. Lack of FDA approval raises concerns about accuracy of supplement labels and manufacturer/distributor accountability. How will we trust that the ingredients on the label accurately reflect the supplement we're ingesting?

Natural Medicines has one of the largest, most comprehensive databases in the United States containing consumer-friendly herbal and non-herbal supplement information. The Dietary Supplement Label Database compares ingredients in thousands of dietary supplements marketed in the United States. This database is accessible through the National Institutes of Health and offers product searches by manufacturer, brand name, and active ingredient. You'll find links to both in the recommended online guides at the end of this article.

Supplements in Your Treatment Plan

Despite recommendations, only 54 percent of individuals taking dietary supplements consulted with their primary care physician, 18 percent consulted with a pharmacist, and 13 percent consulted with a dietitian before use, according to the CRN. Some don't mention supplement usage because it's over-the-counter (OTC), erratic, or seasonal. Others believe that plant-based supplements are "natural," safer, and don't "count" as prescription medications, but this is a dangerous misconception. "Natural" doesn't mean safe, and some herbals are as strong as prescription medications and may be toxic or lethal at high doses. Because herbal supplements may interact with prescription medications, diminish or increase a medicine's effects, or present their own risks or benefits, all treating providers should know about your use in order to provide optimal patient care.

Before taking any supplement, ask your provider's opinion about its safety, risks, and interaction potential. If you have the container, show your provider the label. Are the ingredients and dosage effective? Will the supplement affect your treatment?

I've had clients who used herbal supplements while taking prescription and OTC medications without telling their prescribing doctors, clients who *replaced* their prescription medications with herbal supplements without notifying their prescribing providers, and clients who took herbal supplements even though their surgeons told them to stop two weeks before surgery. Each time, I thanked the client for sharing the information with me, because that showed trust—and for two of them it was probably life-saving.

Take the time to ask the questions. It can save your life. Unfortunately, there are circumstances in which taking herbal supplements can lead to harmful, or life-threatening, events.

Avoid herbal supplements if:

- *You're under eighteen years old or over sixty-five.* Safe herbal supplement doses in children have not been established, and conclusive research into herbal metabolism in older adults is limited.

- *You have multiple health conditions (comorbidities), requiring multiple medications (polypharmacy).* Herbals may affect the medications you take and your medical treatment(s). Your medical doctor may recommend that you completely avoid herbal supplements.

- *You're taking prescription or OTC medications.* Risks for serious side effects or interactions increase when mixed with prescription and OTC medications.

- *You're pregnant or breastfeeding.* Consult with your healthcare provider first, no exceptions.

- *You're having surgery.* Some herbals can affect a patient prior to, during, and after surgery. Discuss herbal supplements with your surgeon and other healthcare providers (including your pharmacist) as soon as you start discussing surgery.

Systemic Side Effects

As with prescription or OTC medications, herbal supplements have the potential to impact specific or multiple organs and systems in the human body, beneficially or harmfully. Limited studies have evaluated the efficacy and side effects of herbal supplements, but most have been of short duration, without diverse participants. Of course, it would be unethical to intentionally include children, pregnant or lactating women, or the immune-compromised in such studies. Many herbal supplements are generally regarded as safe (GRAS), but other outcomes and results vary, and the wording is important.

As with "natural," "not conclusive" does not mean safe. Some studies are mixed or "not conclusive" in determining an herbal's safety, such as outcomes being inconsistent. However, in researching certain "not conclusively" safe herbal supplements, I found them categorized as "potentially unsafe" elsewhere, notably during pregnancy.

Like some prescription medications, certain herbal supplements may cause toxicity to the heart, liver, and kidneys, as well harm during pregnancy. The herbal list below provides some examples of possible side effects but is not comprehensive due to space limitations.

Herbal Supplement	Possible Side Effects
Autumn crocus *Colchicum autumnale++*	Considered unsafe; birth defects, organ failure, rhabdomyolysis*
Black cohosh *Actaea racemosa++*	Digestive upset, increases effects of estrogen, liver damage
Cat's claw *Uncaria tomentosa++*	Acute allergic interstitial nephritis, infertility risk
Cayenne pepper *Capsicum annuum++*	Avoid before surgery, with blood pressure or blood clotting conditions
Chamomile *Matricaria recutita+*	Drowsiness, vomiting, hypersensitivity reactions. Avoid if using birth control pills or with alcohol.
Chaparral *Larrea tridentata++*	Cystic nephropathy, renal cell carcinoma
Chicory root *Cichorium intybus++*	Contact dermatitis, hives, flatulence, abdominal discomfort; those with gallbladder disease should avoid
Copalchi *Coutarea latiflora+*	Rhabdomyolysis*
Cranberry *Vaccinium macrocarpon++*	Nephrolithiasis** (calcium-oxalate stones)

Herbal Supplement	Possible Side Effects
Devil's claw *Harpagophytum procumbens*++	Cardiac distress, gallstones, glucose imbalance, gastric ulcers; medication interactions with NSAIDs, blood thinners, proton pump inhibitors (PPIs)
Echinacea *Echinacea purpurea*++	Stomach pain, potentially severe allergic reactions
Elderberry *Sambucus nigra*++	Avoid if you have autoimmune disease (MS, RA, lupus) or take immunosuppressants. Raw, unripe berries are toxic.
Ephedra *Ephedra sinica*++	Nephrolithiasis**, seizure, cardiac arrest, stroke, sudden death; banned in USA
Feverfew *Tanacetum parthenium*++	Mouth irritation; may induce labor; impaired renal functioning
Frankincense *Boswellia serrata*+	Impaired renal functioning
Ginger *Zingiber officinale*	Interferes with blood thinners; impaired renal function
Ginkgo *Ginkgo biloba*++	Use leaves only; seeds cause seizures and death
Ginseng *Panax ginseng*++	Edema, heart palpitations, vertigo, mania, liver damage
Goldenseal *Hydrastis canadensis*++	Mouth/GI-system irritation, reduced liver function (rare), dose-dependent toxicity
Guarana *Paullinia cupana*++	Similar to caffeine in high doses (e.g., shakiness, heart palpitations)
Guggul *Commiphora mukul*++	Thyroid dysfunction, clotting problems, rhabdomyolysis*

Herbal Supplement	Possible Side Effects
Horse chestnut *Aesculus hippocastanum++*	Impaired renal function. Avoid if allergic to latex.
Kava kava *Piper methysticum++*	Liver damage/failure; kava interacts with other botanicals; review potential interactions with pharmacist
Licorice *Glycyrrhiza glabra++*	Hypokalemia, hypertension, cardiac arrest, renal dysfunction/failure
Marigold *Calendula officinalis++*	May induce menstruation
Meadowsweet *Filipendula ulmaria++*	Lung spasms, kidney problems, tinnitus
Milk thistle *Silybum marianum++*	Avoid if allergic to plant family or you have diabetes or estrogen-sensitive conditions
Pennyroyal *Mentha pulegium++*	Renal failure, nerve damage, seizures, hallucinations, liver toxicity, death
Red yeast *Monascus purpureus++*	Rhabdomyolysis*
St. John's wort *Hypericum perforatum+*	Medication interactions (birth control, antidepressants), GI upset, anxiety, increased sensitivity to light
Saw palmetto *Serenoa repens+*	Liver damage, pancreatitis (isolated cases). More research into birth defects needed.
Sorrel *Rumex acetosa++*	Nephrolithiasis**
Thunder god vine *Tripterygium wilfordii+*	Renal failure, cardiac dysfunction, reduced fertility (males), bone density loss, hair loss, respiratory infections, toxicity risk

Herbal Supplement	Possible Side Effects
Turmeric *Curcuma longa*	Gallbladder problems, acid reflux, slow blood clotting, impaired glucose control, diminished renal functioning
Valerian root *Valeriana officinalis*	Heart palpitations, vivid dreams (nightmares), headaches, dizziness
Vervain *Verbena officinalis*++	Hypertension, early contractions during pregnancy, impaired iron absorption. *Do not use with blood thinners.*
Willowbark *Salix daphnoides*+	Reduces blood flow to kidneys. Slows blood clotting.
Wormwood oil *Artemisia absinthium*++	Rhabdomyolysis*, tonic-clonic seizures, acute kidney injury
Yellow dock *Rumex crispus*++	Laxative, nephrolithiasis**
Yellow oleander *Thevetia peruviana*++	Multisystem organ failure, death
Yohimbe *Pausinystalia yohimbe*++	Proteinuria, progressive renal failure, increased heart rate, hypertension, anxiety, antidepressant interaction; dangerous in high doses long-term

*   Breakdown of muscle tissue that results in kidney damage

** Kidney stones

\+   Avoid during pregnancy

++ Avoid during pregnancy and breastfeeding

Herbal Supplement Safety Tips

- Always consult with your healthcare provider or pharmacist before taking any herbal supplements. They'll inform you of the latest safety and risk information. Virtual and online visits allow you to still "meet with" your provider even if you are unable to leave your home.

- Investigate before purchasing. Don't rely on the supplement's marketing. Find objective, current, evidence-based research to evaluate any reported claims. Refer to the resources section at this end of this article for reliable sites that allow consumers to make informed choices about herbal supplements.

- Remember that "natural" doesn't necessarily mean safe and effective. Herbal supplements are regulated only for manufacturing standards; safety and effectiveness are not guaranteed!

- Choose your brand wisely. Look for label certification that indicates independent quality testing, such as ConsumerLab.com or US Pharmacopeia Convention (USP).

- Check FDA updates periodically. The FDA lists supplements under regulatory review or linked with adverse effects online (see recommended online guides).

- Contact the manufacturer for questions about a specific supplement. Supplement labels must include the manufacturer's contact information. Request supplement ingredients, data supporting their supplement claims, or data on its safety and effectiveness.

- Follow the supplement's instructions. Do not exceed the recommended dosage and duration. Track your intake.

- Notify the FDA to report supplement safety concerns. To contact a consumer complaint coordinator, visit www.fda.gov/Safety/ReportaProblem/Consumer ComplaintCoordinators.

General Consumer Recommendations

For some, herbal supplements may benefit overall health and well-being when medically approved, but understanding the risk of any supplement's side effects allows the individual to make an informed decision about taking it prior to purchase.

Many forms of media inundate the public with inaccurate claims about "miraculous" health-related products, and I'm asked about them daily. Follow these tips to help you decipher fact from fiction:

- Look past the headlines. Products that claim they "work better than X," with X being a healthy eating and exercise plan for weight loss, are often misleading or flat-out wrong. You know the saying: if something sounds too good to be true, it usually is.

- Avoid "always" and "never" advice about eating, weight, or health. For some, restrictive eating plans may lead to nutrient deficiencies and disordered eating patterns down the road. Buyer beware!

- Question unrealistic promises and claims. Descriptive phrasing like "miracle pill," "totally safe," or "sleep the fat/wrinkles away" are glaring red flags to avoid that product.

- Anecdotal evidence ("a real-life story") isn't scientific proof. Even your own provider's endorsement is no guarantee that anyone else would experience the same results from that product.

- Review qualifications and credentials of quoted experts. Celebrity endorsements, while attention-grabbing, don't qualify as expertise in a medical or nutrition-related area of study. As a dietitian, it's frustrating to witness clients struggle with recommendations from a celebrity doctor on television with zero nutrition training endorsing multiple (contradictory!) nutrition-based products.

It's said that with age comes wisdom. Indelible memories of young adulthood within the Generation X experience will always blend amazement, sarcasm, and nostalgic longing with regret. I'll remain befuddled that the term most associated with Gen X was *slacker*. Unsurprisingly, being misunderstood remains a common thread between Gen X-ers.

Though grunge isn't dead, most of its primal voices are now silent. There are echoes now and then. But like those long-gone days of heroin chic, dangerous assumptions about herbal supplements should be avoided; such unsupported beliefs can be as lethal as heroin to the uninformed or misled. Come as you are, but live and learn.

These pages are my sincere effort to positively impact the lives of others, with the goal of leaving a lasting legacy of my own. Though I don't wield a musical instrument, I'm nevertheless inspired to walk a path that shadows the irreplaceable footsteps of sorely missed musical and lyrical icons that I was both blessed and cursed to momentarily experience in real time. My voice is now used to educate but remains forever altered by a sensitive, troubled man who often screamed himself hoarse to express his pain to everyone around him, those who didn't bother to listen, until he was devastatingly, irreversibly, gone.

Fully using one's voice for positive change means knowing when to be silent and listen, allowing others to be heard, even when it's painful.

I encourage you to ask the necessary questions to ensure your own health, dear reader, and believe these words will assist you. I appreciate the opportunity to share them with you. Hopefully they're helpful. If not . . . all apologies.

Recommended Online Guides

Label Wise: A Guide to Understanding Supplement Facts: www.belabelwise.org

National Center for Complementary and Integrative Health (NCCIH). Herbs at a Glance: nccih.nih.gov/health/herbsataglance.htm

NIH MedlinePlus Database of Herbs and Supplements: medlineplus.gov/druginfo/herb_All.html

Resources

"Dietary Supplements." United States Food & Drug Administration (FDA). Last modified August 16, 2019. www.fda.gov/food/dietary-supplements.

"Dietary Supplements—Safe, Beneficial and Regulated." Council for Responsible Nutrition (CRN). Accessed September 14, 2020. www.crnusa.org/resources/dietary-supplements-safe-beneficial-and-regulated.

"Food, Herbs, Supplements." Natural Medicines. Accessed September 14, 2020. https://naturalmedicines.therapeuticresearch.com/databases/food,-herbs-supplements.aspx.

"Information for Consumer on Using Dietary Supplements." United States Food & Drug Administration (FDA). Last modified August 16, 2019. https://www.fda.gov/food/dietary-supplements/information-consumers-using-dietary-supplements.

"2019 CRN Consumer Survey on Dietary Supplements: Consumer Intelligence to Enhance Business Outcomes." Washington, DC: Council for Responsible Nutrition (CRN), 2019. www.crnusa.org/2019Survey.

"Using Dietary Supplements Wisely." National Center for Complementary and Integrative Health. Last modified January 2019. https://www.nccih.nih.gov/health/using-dietary-supplements-wisely.

"Vitamins & Supplements." Consumer Reports. Accessed September 15, 2020. www.consumerreports.org/vitamins-supplements/vitamins-and-supplements-natural-health/.

Herbs for the Urinary Tract

⫷ Holly Bellebuono ⫸

Antibiotics are the main treatment for urinary infections and other common urinary tract issues, but many people find herbs are effective as well. When working with herbs for the urinary tract, I like to think in terms of "action." An herb's action is what it does: simply put, the action is the effect upon the body. For instance, the action astringent tones, tightens, and dries tissues; you would use this in cases that are oozy, wet, and blistery. The action emollient is the opposite: it soothes and moistens tissues, and you would use this in cases that are parched, dry, and inflamed.

The urinary tract is prone to a number of common yet infuriating and often painful conditions, such as itching, infection, and burning, that usually respond well to herbs. Other conditions, such as yeast (*Candida albicans*), are trickier but can still be successfully addressed with herbs and diet. The best way to address a condition is to understand the herb's actions—here, we'll explore a variety of actions and herbs that possess these actions, and then we'll see sample recipes for specific conditions.

Remember that symptoms are the body's response to something wrong; don't ignore your body's signals. Fever, blood in the urine, dizziness, and other alarming symptoms are signs that you should contact a healthcare provider immediately.

Let's explore seven herbal actions that can improve symptoms of urinary tract illnesses and help keep urinary organs healthy:

Astringent

Astringent herbs tone, dry, and tighten. Use astringent herbs to dry up wet, oozy, overly moist conditions.

Best Astringent Herbs

Common garden sage (*Salvia officinalis*) is a strong astringent and relatively safe for both internal and external use. When suffering urinary disorders, brew sage tea to pour into the bath or add sage leaves to recipes for drinking. Sage is also antibacterial and antifungal.

You'll see yarrow (*Achillea millefolium*) listed as having many herbal actions; it is one of the best herbs to address urinary disorders. In addition to stimulating the flow of urine, yarrow also fights infections (including UTI) and helps break fevers. Its bitter taste stimulates digestion, and it heals wounds topically (as a vulnerary), which means it's useful topically on the vagina post-partum. A bolus (or ball) of fresh yarrow leaves inserted can be effective for a yeast infection. Drink yarrow tea either hot (for a fever) or cold (for urinary disorders). Cool or body-temperature yarrow tea can be used as a douche for UTIs and yeast infections.

Other Astringent Herbs: Witch hazel; raspberry leaf, root, and bark; lady's mantle; wild geranium / cranesbill; sweet fern

Diuretic

A diuretic herb encourages the body to produce more urine and increases both flow and quantity of urine.

A diuretic will make you pee. When you're drinking coffee on a road trip, this can be inconvenient. But when you're suffering with a kidney stone, for instance, or dealing with a urinary tract infection (UTI), an increase in the quantity of urine passing through the kidneys and ureters can speed the passing of a kidney stone or help the healing of an infection.

Best Diuretic Herbs

Yarrow (*Achillea millefolium*). See page 140.

Stinging nettle (*Urtica dioica*) is a delicious food herb that serves as a nutritious dietary vegetable, a soothing tea, and a medicine. Cooked or dried, the leaves lose their sting, making it available to be eaten or brewed. Nettle tea is cooling, soothing, slippery, diuretic, and mildly laxative. Drink it freely during illness—especially when dealing with a hot, inflamed condition such as a urinary tract infection—and consider it as a douche for the same symptoms.

Other Diuretic Herbs: Coffee, tea, pipsissewa, valerian, uva-ursi, dandelion

Demulcent

A demulcent herb creates a soothing, cooling feeling internally, particularly in the mucous membranes of the digestive / gastrointestinal tract.

Demulcents help when dealing with stomach ulcers and other painful, hot conditions that are soothed by cooling, mucilaginous herbs and foods. Demulcents are also helpful for hot, painful coughs, and by similar action, for UTI and kidney stone passage.

Best Demulcent Herbs

One of the ultimate soothing herbs, licorice (*Glycyrrhiza glabra*) is sweet, slippery, and cooling. Like oats (*Avena sativa*) and lavender (*Lavandula* spp.), it can soothe hot and angry emotions in addition to tissues. Licorice tea can be drunk cool or hot, is best used for short periods of times, and should be avoided by pregnant women.

Easy to harvest, plantain (*Plantago major, P. lanceolata*) is plentiful and safe. Collect this weed's leaves, smash them with a rock or a mortar and pestle, and simmer in a pan of water. The water will thicken to a slippery, slimy consistency, which is soothing either internally or externally on a wound or burn. I've used plantain in sitz bath preparations for women who have just given birth; its soothing qualities ease tissue tears and relieve inflammation.

Other Demulcent Herbs: Comfrey, coltsfoot, mallow

Antispasmodic

These herbs contain compounds that reduce or ease muscle spasms, jerks, and pain associated with smooth muscle or skeletal muscle spasm.

Herbs that reduce spasms throughout the body can be useful when dealing with pain in the urinary tract. Uterine spasm can be caused by gas, bloating, constipation, menses, kidney stones, and other causes, and continued spasm should be evaluated by a healthcare professional. Antispasmodic herbs are useful for mild spasms and are especially prized by midwives for pregnancy and labor.

Best Antispasmodic Herbs
Cramp bark and black haw (*Viburnum opulus* and *V. prunifolium*) have been long valued to reduce spasms in the uterus. The bark and roots of these shrubs can assist with minor urinary spasm and pain. Use as a tea or douche.

Especially when the pain or spasm is due to anxiety, St. John's wort (*Hypericum perforatum*) is most helpful for facial tics or nervous twitching, though it can also assist with uterine pain in those for whom emotions or anxiety increases the symptoms.

Other Antispasmodic Herbs: Jamaican dogwood, elecampane, spearmint

Antilithic

Antilithic herbs help the body expel "gravel" or stones from the kidneys and bladder; they "soften" the tissues of the urinary system and gastrointestinal tract.

Antilithics are traditional remedies without much modern scientific backing; today, diet plays a large part in keeping stones at bay, and dietary wisdom includes cutting oxalates from the diet (such as peanuts, wood sorrel, spinach, chocolate, beets, and sweet potatoes) as well as reducing salt intake.

Best Antilithic Herbs

Uva-ursi (*Arctostaphylos uva-ursi*), also called bearberry, is a low-growing ground cover that produces leaves that are diuretic, anti-inflammatory, and traditionally antilithic. Brew a tea of the leaves and use only temporarily, as long-term use is not advised.

Corn silk (*Maize* spp.) is easy to harvest—straight off the corn cob when shucking it. The silks are traditionally used as a diuretic and, probably because of this obvious action, have been used as antilithics. Brew a strong tea, cool it, and sip throughout the day to relieve kidney stone pain, UTI symptoms, and bladder infection.

Other Antilithic Herbs: Usnea, joe pye weed, hydrangea

Antimicrobial

This is my catchall phrase for a range of actions: antibacterial, antiviral, antifungal, and antiparasitic. Some of these herbs directly kill pathogens on contact; others assist the immune system's defenses to kill them.

Urinary tract infections are usually bacterial infections that impact the bladder, urethra, or (more seriously) the kidneys. Symptoms include pain, fever, burning when urinating, blood in the urine. Determine which antimicrobial herbs may be called for, and use them internally as tinctures, capsules, or hot teas or as douches or boluses.

Best Antimicrobial Herbs

When you have a UTI or a yeast infection, eat more garlic (*Allium sativum*)—preferably raw, as much as your stomach can tolerate. A clove of garlic can be used (very carefully) as a bolus, which means wrapping it in gauze or cheese cloth and inserting it into the vagina. Leave in for no more than an hour, and wash the hands before inserting and after removing.

The multi-action herb yarrow (*Achillea millefolium*), already discussed, shows up again as a germ fighter. Drink the tea, use the tincture, or create a warm rinse for the exterior of the vagina to soothe and fight infection.

Traditionally used to fight fungal infections, the flower of calendula (*Calendula officinalis*) is valued for fighting *Candida albicans*, the fungus that causes yeast infections and thrush. Young girls often get urinary tract infections and yeast infections; calendula makes a strong tea for them to drink or a bath to sit in.

Other Antimicrobial Herbs: Oregano, thyme, echinacea, sage

Antipruritic

Antipruritic herbs relieve itching. Many emollient herbs also relieve itching; these are often steeped in vegetable oil to make a medicinal oil or salve to place on the skin for insect bites or poison ivy. In the case of urinary health, these herbs can relieve symptoms of pain, inflammation, and itch.

Best Antipruritic Herbs

Chickweed (*Stellaria media*) is a lovely edible spring herb that makes its way into our salads. Its cooling effects make it useful in salves or oils to use on reddened skin and inflamed tissues.

Prized for its safe healing of children's fevers and runny noses, elderflower (*Sambucus canadensis*) blooms on the elder tree in the spring; if it is not harvested, the flowers become the elderberries, used for cough and baked into cobblers. Elderflower tea is cooling and can be used as a douche or a bath; it can also be infused into oil to be applied to the exterior of the vagina.

Other Antipruritic Herbs: Calendula, mallow, violet

Sample Recipes

Kidney Stone Tea

Of course, working with a healthcare practitioner to monitor kidney stones is important. Use this recipe to brew teas that can be drunk daily for up to 3 weeks to ease pain and hasten the passage of the stone.

> 2 parts dandelion leaf
>
> 1 part corn silk
>
> 1 part parsley leaf, mallow root, or plantain leaf
>
> ½ part willow bark

Urinary Tract Healing Tea

For a mild infection or recurring infections, be sure to adjust the diet to exclude sugars (alcohol, sweets, bread/carbs, and fruit). Add garlic to the diet. Use this recipe to brew teas that can be drunk daily for up to 3 weeks to ease burning and strengthen the immune system. Drink the tea in addition to using douches vaginally or sitting in hot herbal baths.

> 2 parts uva-ursi
>
> 1 part yarrow
>
> 1 part turmeric or corn silk
>
> ½ part ginger

Yeast Infection Tea or Douche

For a mild infection or recurring infections, be sure to exclude sugars (alcohol, sweets, bread/carbs, and fruit) from the diet.

Add garlic. Use this recipe to brew teas that can be drunk daily for up to 3 weeks to ease burning and itching and to combat the fungal infection. This recipe can also be used as a douche or bath.

2 parts calendula

1 part yarrow

1 part meadowsweet or echinacea

½ part sage

Topical Itch Oil

Apply this oil topically to ease itching and burning. Wash hands prior to and after application. Make only a small amount as this bottle is for a specific purpose and should not be used for other itching, such as bug bites or poison ivy. Discard when no longer needed.

½ cup minced fresh or dried herbs (choose any):

calendula flowers

chickweed herb

yarrow leaves and flowers

St. John's wort leaves and flowers

violet leaves and flowers

½ cup light vegetable or nut oil (safflower, sunflower, almond)

Mince the herbs and add them to a small saucepan. Add the oil. Heat gently and stir for 20 minutes. Strain the herbs and discard. Reserve the oil in a small jar. Use topically by applying with the fingers or a cotton ball.

Kitchen Co:

~ Charlie Rainbow Wolf ~

I've always been a bit of a do-it-myself kind of gal. Back in the dark ages, when I was still in high school, someone gave me a Yardley oatmeal and lavender facial scrub. It was prettily packaged in a vintage-looking cardboard canister. My young self was very impressed by it—but I was even more intrigued by the idea that maybe this was something I could make myself.

I drove my dad's old Chevrolet land yacht to the library (that thing was so big it got a whopping eight miles per gallon) and checked out every book I could find on herbs and herbal preparations. I discovered a whole world of things I could make for myself simply from household

.edients at a fraction of their commercially produced and
.eatly packaged cousins. This was the start of what was to
become one of my lifelong passions.

The Equipment

Before jumping straight into making your own kitchen
cosmetics, there are some basic guidelines and pieces of
equipment to become familiar with. The main one is to have a
separate set of utensils and containers, ones that are not going
to be used with food products. It goes without saying that most
kitchen cosmetics are completely safe, because they're very
often made from grocery items. It's still not pleasant to have a
faint taste of soap running through the mashed potatoes!

The tools used do not have to be fancy. I use a ninety-
nine-cent blender I picked up from a charity shop and a set of
knives and other utensils obtained from Freecycle. Use what's
on hand; just remember to keep it separate from food prep
where possible, to avoid any potential unpleasant aftereffects.

Recommended Cosmetic-Making Equipment	
Blender	While I don't always use my electric blender, it is handy—particularly when it comes to milling dry ingredients. It doesn't need to be fancy or expensive (see above), but you will need to be able to control the speed. I prefer a jug-type blender to a canister-type food processor for most things, but either will work.
Bowls	Obviously, the ingredients need to be mixed some-where. I prefer glass over plastic; it's more environ-mentally friendly, and there's less chance of cross contamination. My Pyrex bowls were hand-me-downs.

Recommended Cosmetic-Making Equipment	
Jars	The finished product needs to be stored somewhere! I'm a big fan of canning jars—they come in sizes from four ounces to a gallon and are often found going for next to nothing in estates sales or social media marketplaces. Smaller bottles and containers are easily found online and are handy for things like lip salve or special decoctions.
Jugs	These are handy for mixing and pouring. I have my mum's old glass Pyrex jug that holds four cups, and it is ideal for most purposes. Again, I prefer glass to plastic; I wouldn't use plastic in a hot water bath, and the glass jug behaves very well when I cut corners and pop it in the microwave.
Pans	Many times the ingredients need to be heated, particularly in a hot water bath, and thus pans are necessary. I do try to avoid aluminum and cast iron. My favorite one is an old enamel pan that was given to me by one of my best friends' late mother.
Ramekins	These are invaluable when it comes to melting small amounts of ingredients in the microwave or a hot water bath. They're not expensive and are frequently found in thrift stores and charity shops.
Spoons	Any spoon will do. I keep various sizes of old metal spoons, and I do like wooden spoons for making cosmetics too—just seems more natural, somehow. Both metal and wooden spoons can be boiled to be cleaned and sterilized.
Whisk	I've got both a hand whisk and an electric whisk (the electric mixer was another thrift store find), and I use the hand whisk most. It's easier to control and seems to make the finished product less agitated—literally—although that may be my imagination!

I found the more I made my own stuff, the more I got into a rhythm of what I needed and what was just surplus to requirement (like the electric whisk). This is a time-honored practice. I know my ancestors did not have access to electric appliances and microwaves, and they managed just fine. However, as much as I like following in their footsteps and doing things "the old way," I'll take a shortcut when it works!

The Ingredients

Take a look in your cupboard. I bet right now you have enough ingredients to make several kitchen cosmetic creations without even having to go scavenging. For example, the oatmeal and lavender scrub I mentioned earlier? Old-fashioned oats ground to a medium-textured powder in the blender, with lavender flowers added. The end. Of course the commercial product had preservatives added to it. While homemade cosmetics do have a shorter shelf life, they're also made in smaller quantities. I'm a firm believer that fresh is best!

The list below is far from exhaustive. I chose these items for two reasons. The first is because they're readily available and inexpensive. The second is they are things that I use regularly, and I know their value. Please, please, *please* experiment with what you have—you just might reinvent the wheel!

Kitchen Cosmetic Ingredients and Uses	
Almonds	Almonds are a staple in our house, as we cook with them and use them as a snack. In kitchen cosmetics, they're moisturizing and exfoliating. Almond oil might be a bit less familiar, but it is a good carrier oil when making your own products.

Kitchen Cosmetic Ingredients and Uses	
Baking soda	This is sometimes referred to as bicarbonate of soda (NaHCO₃). It's used in cooking as a leavening agent and in cleaning as a mild abrasive. In the fridge, it absorbs odors. In homemade cosmetics, it works as a cleanser, whitener, and exfoliator.
Bananas	There are so many uses for bananas when it comes to making your own facial products! They are moisturizing and soothing, and many people think they smell divine. From face masks to shampoo to lip balm, bananas are a wonderful inclusion in many items.
Coconut oil	Coconut oil has gained popularity over recent years, both in cooking and in homemade beauty products. It might not be something you have on hand at the moment, but it is very easily obtained from online shops and grocery stores, and it's not particularly expensive. Coconut oil is moisturizing, soothing, and one of my go-to oils for salves.
Coffee	Don't throw away those grounds! The zing in a cup of joe is not just limited to what you drink! Coffee is a great stimulant and exfoliator and brings a shine to brown or brunette hair.
Cucumber	Delicious on a salad and cooling in the summer, cucumber is a soothing moisturizer. It's a great ingredient in masks, lotions, and scrubs. If time is short, cucumbers placed on the eyelids provide a quick solution to tired eyes.
Honey	Honey is more than just a sweetener. It's said to rejuvenate the skin and prevent moisture loss. Its slightly acidic nature is believed to make it a mild antibiotic.

Kitchen Cosmetic Ingredients and Uses	
Milk	Whole milk is the best when it comes to beauty products. It has more of the natural nutrients, but note it does tend to spoil a bit quicker. Milk is soothing and nurturing in skin preparations and brings benefits to hair products too.
Oatmeal	This is one of my go-tos when it comes to soaps and scrubs, because it is just so very versatile. I get old-fashioned oats rather than the quick oats. They seem to hold up better; the quick oats have a tendency to mush when water is added.
Peanut butter	No, this isn't nuts! Peanut butter is high in oils and vitamins. This makes it a most appropriate addition to masks and other skin softeners. Choose smooth over crunchy for the best results.
Salt	Salt has long been recognized as both a purifier and a preserver. Meat was salted and cured. It's a natural exfoliant, but use sparingly as it does dry out the skin—which makes it great for use with oily complexions. Natural sea salt is preferred; iodized salt can cause skin reactions.
Sugar	Over the last year or so we've made a valiant attempt to go mostly whole food and plant based with our eating. I had a *lot* of sugar, because before I learned different ways of making jams and jellies (with maple syrup, for example), I made a lot of sugar-based preserves. The solution? I used it for sugar scrubs!
Tea bags	Tea bags or loose tea, black tea or herbal tea, it's all useful in homemade cosmetics! A tea bag over the eyes is a great restorative. Soaking the feet in tea helps eliminate odors. Tea brings out red highlights when used as a hair conditioner.

Kitchen Cosmetic Ingredients and Uses	
Vanilla extract	Vanilla is a great base fragrance for many skin care preparations. It's slightly antibacterial, and it's rich in antioxidants. This makes it valuable for skins of all types and people from all age groups.
Vinegar	Vinegar might not have the most soothing scent, but its inclusion in kitchen cosmetics cannot be overlooked. Vinegar is a solvent, which makes it useful for dissolving soap buildup but does mean that a little goes a long way when it comes to skin treatments. It's a preservative and an acid (its pH level is around 2.5), making it valuable when it comes to foot soaks and deodorants.
Yogurt	For cosmetic purposes, please stay away from the fancy fruity yogurts and look for the plain, un-sweetened, probiotic yogurts—or better yet, make your own! Yogurt is rich in protein and full of natural bacteria and nutrients that have the potential to be very beneficial when eaten or used on the skin. Its smooth, cool texture is soothing too.

The Recipes

These are the recipes I have found to be tried and true, ever since that first oatmeal face scrub I made as a teenager. They're simple and effective and use the common ingredients listed in the table. Follow the basic rules of hygiene, and remember to use separate tools and utensils for cosmetics and food.

Oatmeal Facial Scrub

Here it is, the one that got me started! You will need a blender for this; grinding the oats contributes to the exfoliating action of the scrub. In this instance, food processor blades will work just as well as a jug blender. I'm particularly fond of this recipe because it is dry and does not need refrigeration. Keep it in an airtight glass jar out of heat or sunlight, and it will last on the shelf for several weeks. I find amber canning jars are excellent storage containers for this scrub.

The main ingredient to this is oatmeal. That's it! Place 1 cup old fashioned oats or instant oats in the food processor and pulse until it is a fine powder with a few coarser bits of oatmeal in it. To make the facial scrub, use 1 tablespoon oatmeal in the palm of your hand and add a drizzle of warm water. One cup of oats will make enough for approximately 16 treatments.

What makes this recipe so valuable is its versatility. Add a pinch of salt if your skin is oily. Add those lavender flowers to make it smell nice. Use a bit of honey when mixing it for a moisturising scrub. Ground almonds make the mix incredibly soft, but resist the temptation to eat it—especially if you've used honey as well!

It's possible to add essential oils to this, but I've found two things work best. The first is to ensure the oils are proper food-grade essential oils and not fragrance oils. Fragrance oils might be harsh on the skin. It's always wise to do a skin test before introducing a new ingredient, to ensure no reaction takes place. Also, when adding the oil, add just a drop when the oats are being mixed with the water to ready for use. This means different oils can be used in a heartbeat, and it also means that the dried oats will stay fresher longer.

Banana Face Mask

When is a herb not a herb? When it's a fruit! Technically, a banana is both, but let's not argue semantics. What is certain is that bananas are good for your skin, both inside and out! Eat them, wear them, enjoy them.

The easiest banana face mask is to mush 1 very ripe banana into a cream and then apply it onto the face. This is particularly soothing to skin that's been overexposed to the elements, a bit of sunburn or windburn, perhaps. It's lovely when it's slightly chilled too.

To make the mask even more effective, add a bit of honey to brighten the skin, or perhaps blend in some baking soda and a teaspoon of lemon juice if the complexion is oily or prone to blemishes. A tablespoon of Greek yogurt helps give older skin a bit of a boost. This mask is best made fresh every time it's used, rather than trying to store it—although the ripe banana mash can be frozen for up to 3 months.

Coffee Face Mask

Coffee and yogurt, good enough to eat! This is a wonderfully nurturing and stimulating face mask, a real pick-me-up for those times when fatigue or listlessness threaten to encroach on the day. The lactic acid in the yogurt helps break down dead skin cells, the roughness of the coffee grounds acts as an exfoliant, and caffeine helps bring a natural glow to the skin.

You won't need much for this: a scoop of the coffee grounds from the morning's perk and a scoop of natural yogurt. Mix them well, then apply to the face. Gently massage for 2–3 minutes, then leave another 10–12 minutes before rinsing off. This—like the banana mask—is best made fresh every time it's used.

Sugar Scrub

I used to work with a woman whose husband was a mechanic, and *he* taught me this recipe—he said it was the only thing that would get the dirty engine oil out of his skin. I was skeptical, but it really does work, and it's so very simple. Mix white sugar with cooking oil in the palm of the hands, scrub, and wash off!

Over the years I've tweaked this a bit . . . a lot! I have found that brown sugar is softer and less abrasive. I've found that other oils add different nutrients. The result is the same though: this removes stains from the hands, the brown sugar scrub exfoliates the face, and turbinado sugar, with its coarse grains, is ideal for use as a body scrub. Turbinado also has the most minerals as it is the least processed. I've used demerara sugar in body scrubs too.

Different oils yield different results, and even though I have tried many of the more easily obtained cosmetic oils (peach kernel, sweet almond, jojoba, etc.), I've found that for a scrub, it doesn't make a *lot* of difference. Cheap cooking oil for a hand scrub is fine, but a more natural oil—such as olive oil, walnut oil, or coconut oil—somehow brings a more luxurious feel to body products. Use what is on hand, and then start to experiment.

The basic body scrub recipe is 1 cup sugar and 3 tablespoons oil. My go-to is soft brown sugar and olive oil; experiment to find what works best for you. I like the smell of it just the way it is, but essential oils, vanilla bean paste, a drizzle of lemon juice (orange juice makes it smell wonderful), or up to 6 drops of essential oil make suitable additions.

Add the oil to the sugar, not the other way around. Too much oil and the sugar will dissolve; it needs to stay grainy. I always know I've got the right texture for the light brown sugar when the mixture makes me think of wet sand at Fleetwood beach. To use it, apply it to slightly damp skin and rub in a circular motion, then rinse thoroughly. This will keep stored in an airtight container for up to 1 month, and can be used 3–4 times a week to promote healthy, glowing skin.

Insect Repellant

I'm not a fan of chemicals on my skin, so when the warm, humid weather arrives and the bugs start to find me tasty, I resort to homemade bug deterrent. The one I use is moisturizing and doesn't smell nasty to most people, but when it's applied regularly, the bugs do seem to look elsewhere for their meal. Its key ingredients are found in the kitchen cupboard, but I do add others from the health food shop to give it some extra welly.

The concoction that is in my cupboard at the moment is a mixture of vanilla extract and lemon juice in a jojoba oil carrier. I have also added tea tree and eucalyptus oil to this, but then, I do seem to be overly prone to bug bites. My husband just uses straight-up vanilla extract and does fine on it.

The carrier oil is the key. A light-textured oil, rather than a thick one, is preferred. I've used fractionated coconut oil before today. Add the oil mixture to the same volume of water, and shake it up before applying. There are no harsh chemicals in this mixture, and the oil keeps the skin soft.

Experiment at Home

There are many other ways of using kitchen ingredients for cosmetic purposes. Entire books have been written on this topic, and of course there are many other items to be made from simple kitchen staples—bath salts, bath bombs, toners, moisturizers, and others too numerous to name—with maybe a few other natural ingredients added to provide a desired texture or treat a specific area or ailment. I encourage you to dip your toe into the experience with one of these ideas, and then experiment to see what works for you. You might just find a new passion!

Further Reading

Campion, Kitty. *The Handbook of Herbal Beauty.* London: Random House, 1995.

Donnan, Marcia. *Cosmetics from the Kitchen.* New York: Holt, Rinehart & Winston, 1972.

Norn, Jan. *Kitchen Cosmetics: Recipes for Making Your Own Skin Care Products.* Canada: 3norns Press, 2002.

Rose, Jeanne. *Jeanne Rose's Herbal Body Book.* New York: Perigee, 1976.

———. *Jeanne Rose's Kitchen Cosmetics.* New York: Perigee, 1986.

Supercharge Your Immune System with Adaptogenic Herbs

≫ Kathy Vilim ≪

On a recent summer morning, I stopped by my friend Gene's house to see if he wanted to go for a walk. When I arrived, he was in the middle of making his daily green juice. I watched as he added kale, cucumbers, beets, celery, ginger, and turmeric. He then topped it off with this light brown powdery substance I had never seen before. Gene explained it was ashwagandha and that it provided numerous health benefits, including more energy, relief from depression, better quality of sleep, and superior immune functioning. I then learned ashwagandha is an adaptogen that has been used in Ayurvedic medicine for centuries, long before the term *adaptogen* was put in use.

Nature has given us an endless array of plants with therapeutic value. There are plants that aid every ailment, from runny nose to acid indigestion and from fever to menstrual pain. Everything we need for medicine is right here for us. But instead of taking one herb for this problem and another tincture for that, powerful adaptogenic herbs can treat the whole body. They do this by helping your body fight off stress. When a body is stressed, it can get sick.

Stress can be psychological or nutritional. Either type of stress can depress natural immune system functions. Chronic stress is a major concern in today's world. Your lungs may be stressed from polluted air. You may suffer chronic nutritional stress from mineral-deficient soils, polluted water, and chemical exposure. Your body may be stressed due to lack of deep sleep, which can be caused by urban light pollution. In addition, there is emotional stress brought on by modern-day problems.

Adaptogenic herbs are herbs that do just what the name suggests: they adapt. They work with our body, scouring the terrain, if you will, for signs of imbalance and going about normalizing it!

For thousands of years, humans have turned to these adaptogenic herbs for help balancing their physical bodies, as well as finding calm for their minds. While most of us are familiar with adaptogens from India and China, no matter where in the world you live, plants with adaptogenic benefits can be found growing in the wild.

If we look at Indigenous people the world over, we see they have been using these traditional herbs routinely as medicine. In North America, for example, the Indigenous peoples used American ginseng, *Panax quinquefolius*. American ginseng favors the forests of the Eastern United States. If you live between Missouri and New York, American ginseng could be growing in the wild right in your neighborhood. You can check for natives with a plant finder online.

I am going to talk about some of the best-known adaptogens and where they can be found in nature. As always, consult your primary healthcare provider before beginning any herbal regimen.

Astragalus, *Astragalus mongholicus*

Used for over a thousand years in Traditional Chinese Medicine (TCM), astragalus is a perennial plant native to Korea, Mongolia, and parts of China. *Astragalus mongholicus* (syn. *A. membranaceus*) is commonly known as *huang qi* in Chinese and Mongolian milkvetch in English.

Astragalus is a prominent member of the Fabaceae (pea) family. While there are a few thousand different species of astragalus around the world, *A. mongholicus* is the species best known for medicinal properties. The plant can be grown in USDA zones 5 through 9 in sandy soil. It will reach three to four feet in height, growing white or yellow flowers in summer. The roots are the part of the plant that has all the medicinal power. It is usually four years before the roots have reached maturity, giving astragalus its best performance.

Astragalus stimulates every part of the immune system. It boosts immunity by strengthening the flow of life force energy, known in TCM as *qi*. Additionally, astragalus has anti-inflammatory effects, can lower blood pressure, and can lower blood sugar levels.

In today's world, cancer is of big concern. In TCM, cancer care and prevention is called *fu zheng*. It is based on the idea of using your body's own natural immune system. One of the main herbs used in *fu zheng* therapy, astragalus has been shown to increase interferon levels and activate your body's natural killer cells. In conjunction with acupuncture, astragalus can help give patients energy and relieve discomfort from chemotherapy.

In China astragalus is used in daily cooking. It can be added to stews or smoothies. The dried root can be made into teas and is found in many herbal tonics. The people of China have also benefitted from astragalus's antiaging effects.

Siberian Ginseng, *Eleutherococcus senticosus*

Siberian ginseng (*Eleutherococcus senticosus*), arctic root (*Rhodiola rosea*), and schisandra (*Schisandra chinensis*) are some of the most researched adaptogens from the Arctic region. All three of these are herbs that work to counteract stress, which is known to cause harm to neurological, endocrine, and immune systems.

Used for thousands of years in TCM, *Eleutherococcus senticosus* is not in the same genus as American ginseng or Asian ginseng (*Panax*). A small thorny shrub bearing berries, Siberian ginseng prefers to grow in coniferous forests, close to the forest floor. A native of Russia and East Asia, it is hardy to cold temperatures of 5 degrees Fahrenheit (-15 degrees Celsius) and tolerates poor soil.

Alexander Panossian and Georg Wikman explain in their paper in the research journal *Pharmaceuticals* that when Russian researchers began to look for a competitive edge for their athletes in the late 1940s and 1950s, they discovered Siberian ginseng helped ward off stress and fatigue and improved athletic endurance, including increased oxygen uptake. In addition,

Siberian ginseng acted to improve the quality of sleep and relieve some depression. Russian researchers mixed this herb with schisandra and arctic root to achieve exceptional performance and mental alertness for their athletes. Their studies continued with work on healing colds, flu, and herpes.

Arctic Root, *Rhodiola rosea*

Rhodiola rosea (Arctic root) has been used for centuries by people in northern cultures around the world, from Chinese and Mongolian emperors to the Vikings of Scandinavia.

This low-growing arctic plant thrives in extremely cold climates. Arctic root can grow in rough, rocky soil, making it perfectly suited for mountainous areas. Though arctic root can be found growing in Russia, China, and other northern regions, I was amazed to learn there are different active chemical compounds in the roots that vary depending on where the plants are growing. Arctic root's strong roots keep the plant firmly anchored, despite windy living conditions. It is a tenacious plant with pretty yellow flowers. Arctic root is also commonly known as roseroot due to the roots' roselike smell.

Arctic root was used in Eurasian medicine to combat stress and relieve anxiety. As previously stated, in the 1950s, Russians took a long look at Arctic root as an adaptogen for its athletes in conjunction with their research on Siberian ginseng. They found they could safely substitute these herbs for steroids.

Both the leaves and shoots of Arctic root are edible. Arctic root is better when mixed with other greens in a salad, as it can be pretty bitter. One amusing use I found for this herb is as a flavoring for Russian vodka. To make an infusion for flavored vodka, combine ½ cup sliced and dried Arctic root with 1 quart vodka in a glass jar. Keep in a dark place for a few days to infuse. These jars make excellent gifts!

Schisandra, *Schisandra chinensis*

This herb, native to Russia and China, is a true adaptogen. Schisandra helps boost physical endurance, improve energy, and stabilize blood sugar levels. Adaptogens have the ability to help reduce the effects of stress on the body, and schisandra does this by reducing the number of stress hormones in the bloodstream. According to WebMD, the herb has been found to benefit the mind as well, including better coordination and concentration.

The fruit of *Schisandra chinensis* is commonly called magnolia berry or five-flavored fruit. Schisandra's berries grow on deciduous vines native to Russian and Manchurian forests. Hardy to zone 4, the plant likes moist, well-drained soil and a shaded location. In order to bear fruit, schisandra requires both male and female plants to be planted together.

The herb schisandra has long been a staple in TCM, in which schisandra is believed to be beneficial to *qi*, the life force energy found in all living things. It has a positive impact on the heart, lungs, and kidneys. Schisandra's seeds also contain healthy lignans that improve liver function. When combined with Arctic root and Siberian ginseng, it helps improve concentration, attention, speed of thinking, and endurance, making it an essential adaptogen for athletes.

Schisandra's berries have a flavor that is popular for juicing. Its purple-red berries have all five tastes (sweet, salty, bitter, pungent, and sour) which represent the five elements of TCM (earth, water, fire, metal, and wood).

Ashwagandha, *Withonia somnifera*

Perhaps the most important herb of Ayurvedic medicine is ashwagandha. Ashwagandha (*Withania somnifera*) is a small shrub bearing yellow flowers. Also commonly known as Indian ginseng, this perennial herb is a member of the nightshade family. That's right—it's related to tomatoes, potatoes, peppers, and eggplants. Ashwagandha can be found growing in India, North Africa, and parts of Europe.

Ashwagandha translates from Sanskrit to mean "the smell and strength of a horse." Also known as Indian ginseng, ashwagandha helps prevent and treat stress-induced diseases, including arteriosclerosis, arthritis, diabetes, and premature aging. In animal testing published in the *Journal of Ethnopharmacology* and *Molecular Nutrition & Food Research*, ashwagandha has been shown to improve white blood cell counts and reduce tumor growth, promising for chemotherapy patients.

Ashwagandha is a well-established Ayurvedic Rasayana herb. In Sanskrit the word *Rasayana* means "path of essence," an Ayurvedic therapy that offers regenerative ability. In that regard, I was excited to learn that ashwagandha can actually promote the growth of new nerves!

Ashwagandha has a bitter taste, so it is usually added to smoothies with honey. A popular way to prepare this root is as a tea with milk and cardamom. You can make a supercharging juice similar to Gene's by blending the following ingredients: pure spring water, kale, cucumbers, beets, celery, ginger, turmeric, and ashwagandha.

American Ginseng, *Panax quinquefolius*

Most people look to Asia in their search for ginseng, yet American ginseng, *Panax quinquefolius*, has been used by peoples of

North America for centuries. The Cherokee, Iroquois, Mohe-gan, and Potawatomi, among other peoples, used the plant as a tonic that helped treat conditions such as fever and rheuma-tism, according to *The American Journal of Clinical Nutrition*.

A native to the eastern portion of North America, this perennial is a very slow-growing plant. It can take up to five years before the root is ready for harvest. And, I was surprised to learn, most American ginseng is grown specifically for sale to China!

In TCM, unlike ginseng from Asia, which creates heat in the body (yang), American ginseng is cooling (yin). It can be used for stabilizing fever, reducing swelling, and flushing out the digestive tract. Like other powerful adaptogens around the world, American ginseng has been used to improve cognitive function, help reduce risk of cancer, stabilize blood sugar lev-els, and boost the immune system. Today, American ginseng is available in liquid extracts, powders, capsules, and tablets.

Goldenseal, *Hydrastis canadensis*

Goldenseal is a perennial that thrives in the rich, moist soils of the Ohio River Valley and forests of Indiana, Kentucky, and West Virginia, particularly in the Appalachian region. Also a native Missouri wildflower, it can be found growing in rich, moist woods, on slopes, or in valleys, according to the Mis-souri Botanical Garden.

For thousands of years, Native American peoples, such as the Cherokee and the Iroquois, made use of this herb's power-ful medicine for fever, cough, and pneumonia, per *The Ameri-can Journal of Clinical Nutrition*. Goldenseal was used to treat sore throats and mouth sores and to wash the eyes.

By the mid-1800s, physicians in the Ohio River Valley learned of goldenseal's promising medicine from the Native

Americans. Looking to profit from the sale of a prepared concoction, they began to harvest the herb heavily. Though physicians made the herb in every type of pill, liquid, and powder form, the commercial products couldn't match the medicinal effects produced by using the whole plant in its natural state.

Goldenseal's natural forest habitat is threatened: in 1997, goldenseal was added to the endangered species list. Since a crop takes three to five years to mature, not many farmers are jumping at the opportunity to grow it and give wild populations a reprieve from overharvesting.

Goldenseal is naturally rich in alkaloid compounds, which offer antibacterial and anti-inflammatory properties. Antimicrobials are believed to be the main force behind goldenseal's health benefits. Goldenseal can help restore health to mucous membranes, and when brewed into a tea, the leaves of goldenseal can help stabilize fever, reduce swelling, and flush out the digestive tract.

Black Cohosh, *Actaea racemosa*

In North America black cohosh used to be quite common. It was native from New York's Lake Ontario region down to Georgia. Black cohosh, is a tall, upright white-flowered perennial native to much of eastern North America, including Missouri. It can be found growing in rocky woods in the Ozark region. The plant has a gnarled root structure, and this is where the plant's powerful medicine can be found. Like goldenseal, black cohosh is in the buttercup family!

Also like goldenseal, due to black cohosh's popularity, by the 1800s, it had been harvested almost to extinction. Today black cohosh is an endangered species. Only cultivated herbs should be used.

Long used as an adaptogen, black cohosh is said to increase oxygen intake and boost the immune system. The Cherokee have used black cohosh for centuries to stimulate menstruation and treat cough and cold, and they still do today, writes Professor William Setzer of the University of Alabama. For relief from menstrual cramps, the root of black cohosh can be boiled and drunk. This herb can also be purchased in pill or liquid forms.

Black cohosh is also used as a cooling herb for the spleen, stomach, intestines, and lungs. As a true worldwide adaptogen, there are many related Asian species of black cohosh used in TCM to treat infectious diseases.

Purple Coneflower, *Echinacea purpurea*

Echinacea purpurea, commonly called purple coneflower or simply echinacea, is an herbaceous perennial that is native to prairies, meadows, and woodland environments of central to southeastern North America.

Purple coneflowers were used by many different tribes of Indigenous people of North America. Dr. Wallace Sampson shared with WebMD that he traces modern use of echinacea back sixty years, when a Swiss supplement company "erroneously" learned it was used to prevent colds by the people of South Dakota. However, Daniel Moerman writes in Native American Ethnobotony that the Kiowa and the Cheyenne both used echinacea for sore throats, while the Lakota used it for pain medicine.

Echinacea has been used in hundreds of different pharmaceutical products and is popularly used today to treat the common cold. Besides acting as a stress-reducing adaptogen, purple coneflower is also a detoxicant. Having antibacterial properties, the roots and whole plants were used by many tribes in treating wounds.

Echinacea is often taken as a tea. Some people drink it throughout the day safely. It is most effective when taken at the first onset of a cold. Though also available in capsule form, this herb is more effective as a liquid that could reach mucous membranes in the back of the throat.

Maca, *Lepidium meyenii*

For thousands of years high in the Andes mountains, in the cold and inhospitable climate where little else can grow, maca has been harvested for its powers of energy and vitality. *Lepidium meyenii* grows at extreme elevations (11,000 to 11,500 feet) in the Central Andes, in a habitat of intense cold, light, and wind. While maca can be grown successfully in other places, the medicinal root is not as potent as when grown in the harsh altitudes of the Andes, its place of origin.

Also known as Peruvian ginseng, maca has long been a staple in Peruvian kitchens. A plant in the Brassicaceae (mustard) family, it is a tuber, looking similar to parsnip. Maca is cruciferous, and like broccoli, it is known for its cancer-fighting properties. Maca root comes in three colors: red, black, and pale yellow. The red maca is said to be milder and sweeter than the black with perhaps more energy boost.

One of the main benefits of maca is its help in balancing hormones in both men and women. For men, maca supports healthy sperm production. For women, in addition to balancing hormones, maca fights off menstrual problems and supports calcium absorption for strong bones as they age. This adaptogen can also help alleviate chronic stress by controlling cortisol, increasing stamina, boosting energy and endurance (it is used by some athletes and body builders as a supplement), increasing fertility, improving mood (maca contains flavonoids which are thought to reduce anxiety), reducing blood pressure, reducing sun damage (using extracts from the leaves), fighting free radicals (by promoting natural antioxidants such as glutathione), and improving learning and memory.

Maca is a very nutrient-dense plant that grows where little other vegetation can grow. As such, it was a food staple for the Quechua people for centuries. They used maca to make flan, syrups, and liquor. An essential food in Peruvian kitchens still today, it can be made into stews. In addition, there is a long history of its medicinal use as a panacea, also known as Peruvian ginseng. Today in its powdered form, maca root is added to smoothies for that extra kick of energy.

Adaptogens for Immune System Health

Adaptogenic herbs are known to bring balance to our bodies and our minds, which we need now more than ever. Fortunately, all we need to do is look to the past, to ancient methods of healing to find the answers.

I have learned so much about adaptogens since that morning at Gene's house. At seventy-five years old, Gene is strong and healthy. He doesn't even get colds. He attributes his good health to diet, exercise, and generous servings of traditional adaptogenic herbs and mushrooms.

Resources

"Actaea racemosa." Missouri Botanical Garden. Accessed February 15, 2021. http://www.missouribotanicalgarden.org/PlantFinder/PlantFinderDetails.aspx?kempercode=j790.

Agarwal, R., S. Diwanay, P. Patki, and B. Parwardhan. "Studies on Immunomodulatory Activity of Withania somnifera (Ashwagandha) Extracts in Experimental Immune Inflammation." *Journal of Ethnopharmocology* 67, no. 1 (October 1999), 27–35. https://pubmed.ncbi.nlm.nih.gov/10616957/.

Borchers, Andrea T., Carl L. Keen, Judy S. Stern, and M. Eric Gershwin. "Inflammation and Native American Medicine: The Role of Botanicals." *The American Journal of Clinical Nutrition* 72, no. 2 (August 2000): 339–347. https://academic.oup.com/ajcn/article/72/2/339/4729391.

Davis, Jeanine M. "Forest Production of Goldenseal." Agroforestry Notes, no. 16. USDA Forest Service. July 1999. https://www.fs.usda.gov/nac/assets/documents/agroforestrynotes/an16ff05-1.pdf.

"Echinacea purpurea—(L.)Moench." Plants for a Future. Accessed February 15, 2021. https://pfaf.org/user/Plant.aspx?LatinName=Echinacea+purpurea.

"Goldenseal." Gaia Herbs. Accessed February 12, 2021. https://www.gaiaherbs.com/blogs/herbs/goldenseal.

"Hydrastis canadensis." Missouri Botanical Garden. Accessed February 15, 2021. https://www.missouribotanicalgarden.org/PlantFinder/PlantFinderDetails.aspx?kempercode=k570.

Landis, Robyn. *Herbal Defense: Positioning Yourself to Triumph Over Illness and Aging.* New York: Warner Books, 1997.

Moerman, Daniel E. *Native American Ethnobotony.* Portland, OR: Timber Press, 1988. Page 205.

Panossian, Alexander, and Georg Wikman. "Effects of Adaptogens on the Central Nervous System and the Molecular Mechanisms Associated with Their Stress-Protectice Activity." *Pharmaceuticals* 3, no. 1 (January 2010): 188–224. https://www.ncbi.nlm.nih.gov/pmc/articles/PMC3991026/.

Palliyaguru, Dushani L., Shivendra V. Singh, and Thomas W. Kensler. "Withania somnifera: From Prevention to Treatment of Cancer." *Molecular Nutrition & Food Research* 60, no. 6 (June 2016): 1342–53. https://www.ncbi.nlm.nih.gov/pmc/articles/PMC4899165/.

"Schisandra." WebMD. Accessed February 15, 2021. https://www
.webmd.com/vitamins-and-supplements/schisandra-uses-and
-risks#1.

Setzer, William N. "The Phytochemistry of Cherokee Aromatic Medicinal Plants." *Medicines* 5, no. 4 (December 2018): 121. https://
www.ncbi.nlm.nih.gov/pmc/articles/PMC6313439/.

Sinatra, Stephen T. *Optimum Health.* New York: Random House, 1997.

WebMD Health News. "Study: Echinacea Cuts Colds in Half."
WebMD. June 26, 2007. https://www.webmd.com/cold-and-flu
/news/20070626/study-echinacea-cuts-colds-by-half#1.

"What Is Maca." The Maca Team. Accessed February 15, 2021.
https://www.themacateam.com/what-is-maca.

"Which Adaptogen Herb Is Best for You?" Living Alchemy. Accessed
February 15, 2021. https://livingalchemy.com/blog/which
-adaptogen-herb-is-best-for-you/.

DIY
and
Crafts

Projects to Make Your Herb Garden Welcoming to Wildlife

≫ Annie Burdick ≪

The closer we get to nature, the more it rewards us. By gardening, growing new life in our own spaces, we lay down the delicate seeds that will become sprouts and plants and even food. Then we wait. We engage in a delicate dance, letting nature run its course while longing to maintain some control in a place where we have none. We are a part of this planet, as much as the seeds and plants we place in the dirt. We feel this connection with nature, tucked alongside hope that something will come of it, that we will create and sustain small life in our own spaces. These moments of connection are beautiful, they're purposeful, and they remind us how close to the world we really are.

This is why we love to garden. It brings us closer to the heartbeat of our planet. It reminds us daily of the beauty the world creates without any intervention. It's easy to recognize the connection between growing plants and giving a bit of kindness back to nature. The two are inseparable. Any positive connection you make with the natural world is part of repairing it. Though any one person's effect on nature may be small, in a combined effort, we accomplish more than we realize, good or bad. Those of us who garden start a chain reaction.

Your herb garden, whether a small collection of potted plants or a large and flourishing herb-centric oasis, puts you more in touch and in tune with the earth and ecosystem around you. Not only do the herbs you plant offer countless benefits to you—in your cooking, your projects, your herbal remedies, and so on—but they also attract and sustain members of the animal kingdom that live outside your door. There are many small creatures who are attracted to herbs and find them a great source of food and even shelter. The first step to being more wildlife-friendly in your garden is simply having a great variety of plants. But you can take it further. The second half of this article is filled with projects you can do at home to start enhancing your outdoor space and welcoming more local creatures to your garden.

Garden Wildlife

First, let's take a look at who might stop by to share your herb garden with you.

Birds

Birds are classic and lovely garden visitors, and of course you can entice them with some bird feeders and baths (see pages

180–182 for DIY options!), but birds may also be drawn in by a few of the herbs in your garden. They won't typically eat the plants themselves, but they'll be attracted to the seeds dropped by some herbs in autumn, including fennel and angelica, as well as the shelter provided by larger bushes, like mature rosemary. Many dried herbs also provide excellent and healthy additions to traditional bird seed and can even help keep wild birds healthy.

Bees and Butterflies

These are some of the most important wildlife visitors you can attract, and thankfully they're also the ones most drawn to a variety of herb plants. Bees and butterflies are two of the world's most important pollinators, which means they're responsible for the growth of most of the food crops we eat, as well as the flowers and plants around us. They're both facing major population losses. Supporting the health and well-being of the bees and butterflies in your area is one of the best things you can do for the ecosystem. Bees and butterflies are attracted to lavender, borage, sage, thyme, caraway, oregano, chives, and mint, among others.

Beneficial Tiny Insects

You probably have a few insects in mind that you're not fond of. Mosquitoes are pretty universally disliked, while aphids, slugs, and several types of beetles are considered garden pests, munching through massive patches of your plants. One way to support your local food chain without having to spray harmful insecticides is to encourage beneficial insects, like predator insects who feed on these pests, to visit your garden. Some will be attracted to herbs like fennel, valerian, borage, and anise.

Small Mammals

Possibly the most elusive but entertaining guests, small mammal visitors can include rabbits, mice, chipmunks, and of course squirrels. Keep in mind: squirrels don't deserve all the hate they get. Yes, they're messy and steal bird food, but they're part of a functioning ecosystem like any other creature, and they also inadvertently plant many of the trees you see outside around you just by hiding nuts and seeds and forgetting about them. Supporting wildlife in your garden means being friendly to all of it and knowing it will cause a chain reaction!

There are many unsafe herbs for rabbits, so keep that in mind and do your research before planting them low to the ground if you know you have rabbit guests. As for herbs they *can* enjoy, try basil, parsley, dill, comfrey, caraway, and clover.

DIY Wildlife-Friendly Garden Projects

There are countless simple and affordable projects you can do at home to make your yard, garden, or patio into a wildlife-welcoming space. These are a few of my favorites to get you on track to have lots of happy animal visitors in no time.

Upcycled Bottle Bird Feeder

While it's perfectly simple to buy a bird feeder at any garden store, you can also opt to make one yourself for a fraction of the cost with supplies you may already have.

You will need:

> Empty, clean 2-liter bottle
>
> Utility knife
>
> Thin wooden dowels

Ribbon or thin cord

Birdseed blend

Once the bottle is completely clean and dry, carefully use the utility knife to cut two circular holes in each side of the bottle. The holes should be close to the bottom, but leave enough room for a pool of birdseed to collect inside, about 2–3 inches up. Then use the knife to cut several smaller holes in the bottle, across from each other, so you can run a dowel through from one hole to another. These should form a perch that birds can land on to eat the food, so they should be positioned just next to or below the larger holes. Then cut final holes in the top of the bottle and run ribbon or cord through, tying it in a strong knot at the top. Hang this loop from a strong tree branch or hook in a place where birds can safely access it. Fill the bottom portion with bird seed. Remember that some of your dried herb bounty can make a delicious and healthy addition to the seed mix. This includes dried parsley, sage, rosemary, thyme, bee balm, spearmint, lavender, and marjoram.

Creatively Pieced-Together Birdbaths

Again, there is a massive array of birdbath styles for sale at stores and online, but ultimately any birdbath is just a shallow receptacle that holds water and is attached to a sturdy base. That means its a project you can make yourself and be endlessly creative with, particularly with upcycled and vintage supplies.

Here are some potential items you can turn into the "bath" portion of your homemade birdbath:

- Vintage servingware and dishes (think shallow platters, deep plates, decorative bowls, pie or cake pans, and so on)
- Metal garbage can lids
- Repurposed planter saucers
- Decorative ceramic bowls and containers
- Old salvaged sinks and other extra-creative pieces

Here are some items you could use for the base of your homemade birdbath:

- Vintage metal furniture (properly treated for the outdoors)
- Sturdy lamp bases
- Plant stands
- Stacked bricks or existing landscaping features
- Stacked and safely-adhered teacups or pots

The key to this project is thinking outside the box. Spend a day at a thrift shop or antique store and look for unique objects that could be combined to make a practical but unique birdbath. Then be sure to attach them safely. Depending on the items you choose, this may involve super glue, hot glue, cement, or just resting one item on another. Ideally, the bath should have a slope to it, with a depth of half an inch to one inch at the sides and no more than two inches in the center. To keep algae from growing too quickly, replace the water often, add a bubbling or trickling feature, or toss several pennies in the bath.

Squirrel Feeders

Squirrels are also commonly thought of as a nuisance to have around, but truly, being a friend to nature and wildlife means being kind to all parts of it. And it really does reward you. Squirrels offer plenty of benefits to our ecosystem, planting trees and plants and supporting the food chain like all other living creatures. Squirrels get a lot of heat for eating all the birdseed before the birds can, but they're just trying to eat too, and there are plenty of bird feeder styles and solutions you can use to keep squirrels out. You can also aim to distract the squirrels by creating feeders just for them. Squirrels prefer larger offerings like sunflower seeds and nuts. These two feeders are both totally squirrel-specific and will keep their attention away from the bird seed.

Slinky Feeder

This feeder style repurposes a classic toy and requires only three components, including the food itself!

You will need:

A Slinky

Strong ribbon, yarn, or cord

Peanuts or other large squirrel-safe nuts

Start by curling the Slinky up halfway, into a half-circle shape. Thread the ribbon or yarn through the Slinky tube and then tie it in a knot above, leaving a large loop you can use to attach it to a tree branch. Fill the curved bowl that's created with nuts and then hang from a branch or hook where squirrels can reach it.

Mason Jar Feeder

Here is another simple DIY feeder that uses supplies you can thrift or find around the house.

You will need:

    32-ounce mason jar (no lid needed!)

    Fork or spoon

    Thin metal wire

    Nuts or other squirrel food

To put it together, turn the mason jar to one side so it's parallel to the ground. Then place the spoon or fork along the side, with the prongs or end sticking out past the opening of the jar. This will provide a spot for the squirrels to perch and grab food. Wrap the wire around the jar and utensil to attach them together. Then find a fence post or railing where you can attach the feeder. Use more wire to wrap around the jar and post, attaching them securely together. Fill the jar up with peanuts or other squirrel treats.

Safe Garden Spaces for Wild Rabbits

For some gardeners, rabbits are viewed as something of a pest, but if you want to welcome them and sustain a flourishing ecosystem in your garden, there are plenty of ways to do so. Wild rabbits will likely be wary of human-built shelters, but leaving out a pile of brush and leaves for them to hide and take shelter in is a start. You can also just leave a small patch of your yard uncut and unweeded, and they'll seek shelter and food here! Near this pile or patch of yard, you can also set out some fresh water. Then there are the snack offerings. Rabbits are pesky when they eat your garden bounty before you can harvest it, so try to plant in raised garden beds, and then leave fresh herb and veggie scraps near this designated shelter spot. There are some fruits and veggies that are poisonous to rabbits, so avoid avocado, fruit seeds, rhubarb, allium vegetables, and iceberg lettuce. You can leave out plenty of things you may not even use, including beet greens, lettuce ends, herb stems and leftovers, end pieces of carrot, and so on. Start small, with one item at a time, and add a little more as the rabbit visitors get used to the snacks you're leaving.

Three Ways to Attract More Helpful Insects

As mentioned earlier, while some insects are certainly pests, there are plenty of others that do nothing to harm you but plenty to help you. Lots of hero insects spend their days eating pesky bugs like mosquitoes and aphids or helping break down dead biological matter into rich, new soil. Plenty of these handy bugs are already living in your garden, but if you want to make them feel more at home, add one of these options to your yard or garden:

Compost Pile or Bin: A compost pile is a win for everyone. Helpful bugs love it as a source of food and shelter, and you'll love the compost they create in it. You can leave your yard waste and food scraps inside, and over the course of weeks and months, insects will break it down into nutrient-rich compost, which is great for your garden. If you have a compost bin or even want to create a more complex multitiered wormery, you can also buy composting-specific worms, super helpful insects that will break your waste down at crazy speeds.

Log Piles: If you find yourself with logs, branches, or sticks you could get rid of, consider keeping them around. Stacked up in even a small pile in the side of your garden, this is the perfect spot for a medley of insects to find shelter, and they'll also help decompose the wood over time.

Homemade Rockery: A mini rock garden is a simple project to add to your garden. If you plan it out right and do some real landscaping, it can be a beautiful element of your outdoor space. But even if you opt to just pile a few rocks together, perhaps with some succulents and ground cover plants nestled between them, all the nooks and crannies of a rockery make a great home for little insects.

Honeybees alone are responsible for about 80 percent of pollination worldwide. To put it another way, seventy out of the top one hundred human food crops rely on bees to grow. Despite their importance, one in four bee species now faces potential extinction.

Homemade Bee Hotel

When you picture a bee's home, you're probably automatically thinking of a bee hive, right? In reality, there are many thousands of different bee species in the world, in a wide range of sizes, shapes, and living styles. Many bee species are solitary, preferring to roam and live on their own rather than work and live in a hive. For these bees, finding safe spaces to take shelter and lay their eggs is critical to staying alive and continuing their work of pollination. Now that more of us are aware of the need to protect bees, it's easy enough to find and buy a premade "bee hotel" designed for solitary bees. But you can also save some money and enjoy the adventure of making one yourself.

This project allows for a lot of flexibility and creativity, as you can choose what materials to include and the patterns and sections you'll incorporate into your bee hotel. There are a variety of styles out there. Some styles opt for exclusively logs and wood blocks with holes drilled in them, but getting creative and including sections with moss, branches, bamboo, and other natural materials will provide more variety in the hotel and therefore entice a wider variety of bee species, and even other helpful insects.

You will need:

Large wooden crate or similar weather-resistant box with an open side

Logs and wood blocks

Moss, twigs, tree bark, pine cones, bamboo stalks, leaves, and other natural filler material

Drill and drill bits

To start, take your wood crate (or build a box of your own by drilling together several large pieces of wood) and stack up sections within it. Fill parts with logs or wood blocks (with the narrow ends facing outward) and cut them down if they stick out too far. You can fill other sections with other materials you've collected. Then take a drill and make small holes in the outward-facing ends of any logs and wood blocks in your bee hotel. These holes should be less than half an inch in diameter, and you can make as many as you'd like. Many bee species seek out these perfect-size holes for shelter and nesting, as they're very secure from predators.

Solitary bees are very unlikely to sting you, since they're not protecting a hive, but it's always safest to put a bee hotel in a nice secure corner of your yard where you won't get in each other's way.

Fully Functional At-Home Butterfly Oasis

Butterflies are nectar fanatics, constantly seeking out flowers to drink from. While they're less effective pollinators than bees, butterflies still do their fair share of moving pollen around fields of wildflowers and helping our plants grow and thrive. And, like bees, butterfly populations are declining due to human influence on the environment. Knowing that, you may be looking for some way to attract more butterflies to your garden and help keep them strong and healthy while they're there. One project you can do is more of a garden expedition: dedicate part of your garden to be a butterfly oasis. Butterflies are attracted to many herb plants, so that's already a great start. Add some flowering bushes and a few other handy treats and it'll become a true butterfly haven. Here's how:

Start with the Plants: If you want to make it great for wildlife *and* lovely to look at, use a variety of colorful, attractive planters. Use some hanging baskets or find creative ways to upcycle vintage items into flower planters. Then choose a variety of plants. The better plant variety, the more butterfly variety. Also be sure to choose flowers with a range of blooming seasons. Aim for a mix of flowers and herbs, as this will give the garden both beauty and practicality. Here's a list to start with:

- Beebalm
- *Baptisia*
- Yarrow
- Phlox

- Sunflower
- Mint
- Lavender
- Snapdragon
- Verbena
- Daisy
- Butterfly bush

Incorporate a Pedestal for Water: Nestled somewhere within all the plants, include a platform or pedestal where you can put out dishes of water. Use only small shallow plates or dishes and include rocks and small sponges in the water. These will provide places for butterflies to land, and sponges soak up water and make it easier for them to drink.

Set Out Fruit: Some butterfly species also enjoy fruit or even prefer it to flowers. Choose particularly juicy fruits like watermelon, mangoes, and oranges if you can, though most fruits will do. Overly ripe fruit is best, so it works to leave out the fruit you didn't get around to eating! Add fruits to your water platform when you can, and change them out daily to prevent rotting.

Whether you choose one project to try out in your garden or you start to create a full wildlife-friendly haven, you are doing something good for the planet and the creatures that share it with us. Even growing food and plants at home is an amazing start, connecting you to the earth and doing a little to heal it at the same time. If you do decide to leave food and shelter for nimal guests, just know that the time and effort will be worth it, it will be appreciated, and you'll be doing a little extra good for your local ecosystem.

Step Up Your Gardening: Add a Third Dimension with Trellises

⤞ Corina Sahlin ⤝

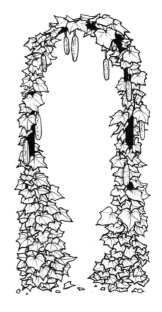

The morning dew feels nice and cool on my feet. Coffee cup in hand, I stroll toward the vegetable garden to pick some kale for my morning smoothie. Something whisks by my head, and I startle, almost spilling my hot drink. Out of the corner of my eye, I detect a bright red sheen flitting by and realize with delight that it's a hummingbird, heading straight for the star jasmine flowers. I planted this jasmine plant ten years ago, and since then it has shot up and climbed to the top story of our house, spreading the scent and beauty of its delicate flowers while also shielding the kitchen window from the hot afternoon summer sun.

Tearing my eyes off the hummingbird feasting on nectar, I start walking but get stopped in my tracks again. A sweet scent makes me look up into the alder tree where the fragrance seems to be coming from. Gently swaying honeysuckle flowers tower over my head, spreading their intoxicating smell from twenty feet above. I planted this honeysuckle start when it was only a tiny baby fifteen years ago, and it's happy here. I marvel at its resourcefulness of using the alder tree as a trellis to climb up on, just as the jasmine is using the rough cedar-shingled side of the house to climb.

A few more steps and I enter the garden underneath the rose-covered arbor my husband built. Old English roses spill over and around it, wafting their scent about like they're in a parade throwing candy with wild abandon.

I marvel at the beans twining their tendrils up our bamboo tepee. I admire the cucumbers neatly clinging to the trellis we built and the peas steadfastly climbing up the hog panel we use as a trellis. Our tomatoes are industriously setting fruit, supported by tomato cages. Squashes travel their way upward on the trellises we erected for them.

Our place is a trellis paradise, and the flowers and vegetables love them. Grab a cup of coffee and sit with me by the rose arbor so I can tell you about trellises. Maybe you can steal some ideas for your own garden.

Growing Vertically

Trellises are your best friends, especially if you don't have a large garden or planting area. When you grow things vertically, you increase your growing space. Instead of sprawling and spreading and thereby choking out other growing things while taking up lots of space, you can train plants up a trellis and conserve space, taming the wildness.

Another benefit of growing plants up off the ground is that they are easier to reach. Instead of crawling on your knees to pick crops hidden by foliage, you can harvest them more easily when they are trellised. Besides, growing vertical crops makes chores like watering, pruning, and fertilizing easier and saves your back!

Trellises also help the plants, since raising them up off the ground improves air circulation and prevents damage from pests and diseases. It keeps them cleaner, because soil doesn't get splashed on your beautiful vegetables when watering or when it rains. And speaking of beautiful: vertical gardening keeps animals from gnawing on crops or digging them up. I used to have unsightly rodent bites on my squashes when I let them grow on the ground.

Vertical garden elements create privacy and the ambience of mystery and surprise. What hides behind the magical green column of pole beans? It's like discovering different rooms in the garden. See how delightfully the espalier of climbing roses hides the view into the neighbor's yard?

Let's talk about my favorite trellises and how to build them, which might be easier and cheaper than you think!

Tepees

In my opinion, this is one of the most romantic options: What's prettier than delicate bean tendrils prettily twining themselves up a bamboo pole tepee? We use bamboo poles because we grow bamboo on our property and have a never-ending supply of poles. You could also use straight branches, other poles, or even PVC pipes, as long as they are at least one inch in diameter and eight feet long.

For one tepee, use three poles. Push each pole about a foot into the ground. Space them in a triangle about three feet apart each, and lean the tops into each other. Then lash or wire the top together with string or wire, so that the tepee feels stable and sturdy.

Plant two to four seeds on the inside of each pole. I tend to plant more seeds than necessary, in case they don't germinate or slugs or birds eat them. If they all germinate, you can always thin them later. As the plants grow, they twine themselves around the poles. They want to grow up! They might need a little help from you, wrapping the tendrils around the poles or maybe even tying them with string if the poles are slick.

We like to use this tepee method for pole beans because they don't get too heavy. If you grow heavy crops like winter squash or even cucumbers on tepees, they might get lopsided and fall over.

Hog Panel Fence Trellis

We grow cucumbers and peas on rigid, heavier-gauge hog panels, which create a lovely and sturdy fence that veggies can climb up on. Don't use chicken wire for this—it's not rigid enough. You want to find galvanized 4-gauge steel panels. They come with variable vertical spacing, with four inches at the bottom and six inches at the top. We found that fifty inches total height works best, because it gives the plants enough room to grow up but is not too tall, which makes them harder to handle.

Depending on how big your growing area is, use steel T-posts every four feet to support the hog panels. We use six foot T-posts and pound them eighteen inches or so into the ground with a sledge hammer or a fence post pounder (also called a T-post driver). It helps to have someone hold the T-post while the other person pounds. Don't hit your helper on the head! (Don't ask me why I know this . . .) When all the T-posts are in, lean the hog panel against them, and attach it to the posts with plastic zip ties, string, or wire.

Sometimes peas grow a little unruly, so I tie them horizontally by attaching a hemp string to one T-post and then pulling it along to the next T-post, which gathers all the green matter closer to the hog panel. I found this helpful when my kids were younger and little hands pulled ripe peas off the vines a little too eagerly.

Whenever possible, use compostable string such as sisal twine, hemp, or jute instead of baling twine or plastic string, because it's so much easier at the end of the season. Instead of having to pull plastic out of the plant material, you can just cut the compostable string off the posts and plop it all in your compost pile.

Field Fencing Trellis

You can use the same concept as the hog panel fence trellis, but instead of the rigid hog panels, use field fencing that comes in rolls. It can be tricky to unroll the rolls and get them to lie straight, and then to cut them with wire cutters to the correct length. But it's an inexpensive option, and many of us gardeners have extra fencing lying around to reuse.

Stepladder-Style Trellis

An easy and quick way to fashion a trellis is to repurpose an old stepladder. Just put it up where you are planting seeds, jump up and down on it for a bit to make it sink into the soil so it's securely attached, and wait for green things to climb up on it soon. Instead of a ladder, build something out of wood that looks like a ladder, prop it up in the garden, plant seeds, and voilà!

Wooden Pallets

If you are looking for an inexpensive or free trellis construction project, look no further than wooden pallets. You can often find them for free behind supermarkets or other big stores. They seem to be everywhere! Haul a pallet to your garden, lean it against a shed, T-posts, or anything that offers support, and you get an immediate gratification boost. Now you only have to wait for seeds to sprout and find their way up this convenient trellis!

By the way: this method works for anything that resembles wooden pallets. I've seen people prop up old bed frames to help roses clamber upward. It's charming!

Trellising Tomatoes

Who doesn't love a juicy homegrown tomato fresh off the vine? The problem is, tomato plants get floppy and heavy when they're ripe with big, red fruits hanging off them. You need to lend them support, and there are several ways to do it.

Our favorite way is field fencing, also known as woven wire fence. We use four-foot high fencing. Cut a five-to-six-foot section with wire cutters. Make this into a cylinder by wrapping the cut ends of the horizontal pieces onto the vertical pieces or by tying it together with wire. Basically, you are making a cylinder you can place over already-planted tomato starts. You can push the tomato cage into the soil a few inches to secure it or use landscape staples, kind of like tent stakes.

*Trellises are your best friend, especially if you
don't have a large garden or planting area. They
increase your growing space, make harvesting easier,
create healthier plants due to improved air circulation,
and keep crops cleaner. They also serve as beautiful
living privacy screens.*

As the tomatoes ripen, you can just reach through the holes in the fence to pick them. It's like a treasure hunt!

If you grow your tomatoes in a greenhouse, another way to trellis them is to simply tie a string above each plant (hanging from the greenhouse roof support), and tie the bottom end of the string to the base of the plant stem loosely. You don't want to girdle the plant. As you keep pruning side shoots, you keep twisting the main leader around the string. Many commercial growers use this technique because it uses vertical space very effectively.

Living Trellis

Don't overlook living trees as organic trellises! We have a large fig tree on the south side of our goat barn. Years ago, I planted a clematis next to it, hoping she would climb up the barn wall in a pretty and dainty fashion. Did she listen to me? No, she didn't. With a mind of her own and a rebellious streak, the clematis threw herself onto the fig tree with wild abandon and has cavorted with him for years, stretching herself upward and making herself comfortably at home all over the tree, who doesn't seem to mind her attention.

Don't let plants like English ivy do this, however. They will girdle the tree and kill it.

Gazebos, Arbors, and Pergolas

We can't talk about trellises without mentioning outdoor structures such as gazebos, arbors, and pergolas. These tend to be more sturdy but time-intensive and more expensive to build than what we have discussed so far. Pergolas are structures consisting of columns that support an open roofing grid of beams and rafters. Gazebos are similar, but they usually have a full roof that provides coverage from the elements. Both offer wonderful support for heavier climbing perennials that need more heft, such as wisteria, climbing hydrangea, kiwi, some roses, hops, and more.

Make sure you erect very sturdy climbing options for these types of plants. We learned this the hard way when we planted a hardy kiwi, a vigorous climber that got incredibly top heavy. One winter, it accumulated lots of snow and got so heavy that it broke the kiwi arbor!

Lots of these plants start out as wispy little things when you first plant them, but if they're happy, they grow into big, heavy, luscious giants that need a tremendous amount of support.

Keep in mind that you need to trim and prune them regularly so they don't take over—like the gorgeous climbing rose that throws herself around the beautiful arbor my husband built. This rose reaches for me and scratches my bare skin every time I try to mow the grass around it. And to think that she started out as a tiny one-foot, one-stemmed dwarf!

Herb Crafts for Children

⤞ Autumn Damiana ⤝

One of the most fulfilling things about working with children is watching them discover the world around them. More than ever it is essential that children are exposed to the outdoors as much as possible, because time, progress, and technology have removed them from the natural world. As an early childhood educator, I have written a curriculum that seeks to bring nature into the classroom as much as possible so that every child can have that connection to it even if they don't have access. Here is a collection of my favorite nature projects I've done over the years.

First, I have a few tips for crafting with children:

1. Arts and crafts are about hands-on experiences, not about "making something." These instructions are just a starting point. Feel free to modify them in any way to accommodate your child. The point is to learn and have fun!

2. Allow your child to do as much as they are able to on their own. You should be there to help direct their experience, not to decide it. You will be surprised what you can learn from each other when you let things unfold spontaneously.

3. Let your child guide you. See what they are interested in, and try not to limit their options. Play and exploration are the tools that children use to learn about the wider world, and they will be more invested if they help with the planning.

4. Please note that the projects are divided by age, but these are just guidelines. If you and your child want to try a craft from a different age group, go ahead!

Ages Two to Four (Preschool)

When you work with very young children, you can use natural elements to create a sensory experience. Run with it and see what happens!

Dried Leaf Glitter

Traditionally a fall project, you can do this any time of the year if you gather the green leaves and give them time to wither and dry. In either case, let your child pick the leaves—they will be drawn to certain ones, and this will make the craft more meaningful.

You will need:

Handful of crunchy dead leaves

White glue

Thick paper or cardboard (construction paper is fine)

Craft glitter (optional)

Collect dead leaves. Let your child break them up in their hands over a large bowl—they will love the sound and the feeling of crushing them. Encourage them to make the leaf pieces as small as possible.

Use the white glue to draw shapes on the paper. Make a smiley face, a star, your child's name, or whatever you like!

Spread the broken leaves over the white glue. Help your child with this step, and periodically shake off the excess leaf pieces like you would with glitter. They can be used again if they are not too covered in glue.

If you wish, you can then repeat the process with actual craft glitter, which is much finer and will stick to the glue in between the leaf pieces.

Herbal Paint Brushes

This is another exploratory activity that can be done with almost any kind of plant matter. Gather herb shoots, flower stems, brushy plants like pine needles or rosemary, or even weeds.

You will need:

Herbs, flowers, or other plants

Several rubber bands

Tempera or finger paint

Large piece of paper (butcher paper is perfect)

Help your child pick out the plant they want to use. Make sure to gather a handful of it.

Bunch the group together and rubber band it in several sections so that it won't come apart.

Have your child dip the "brush" into the paint and let them draw freeform designs on the paper.

This project works best when there are several different "brushes" to choose from. Each one will create different strokes, and you and your child can compare and contrast the resulting patterns.

Seed Shaker

Here is an old craft with a new, herbal twist. Using paper plates, your child will make a tambourine that they can shake for a music and movement activity. For your shaker filling, you can save and dry seeds from melons, squashes, or pumpkins. You can also use rice, lentils, or beans. Chunks of bark will also work when broken into smaller pieces. Or, wait until the plants in your garden go to seed and use those.

You will need:
> Shaker filler
>
> 2 paper plates (any size)
>
> Finger paints, watercolors, or crayons
>
> White glue
>
> Binder clips or clothespins (optional)
>
> Stapler (optional)
>
> Hole punch and yarn (optional)

Collect your shaker filler with your child. This can be done on a walk, in the garden, by drying seeds in the kitchen, or by using dry goods. Help your child pick out filler based on their preferences—you can use size, color, shape, sound, and so on.

Have your child decorate the backs of the of the two paper plates with paints or crayons.

Set one plate facing up and place the filler inside it. Then, squeeze a thick line of white glue around the plate's rim.

Place the other plate face down on the first one, making sure that the rims of the plates touch. This will glue your shaker together. You can use binder clips or clothespins to press the plates together while the glue dries, or staple around the edges for extra support.

If you want to add a component that will help develop fine motor skills, punch holes around the edge of the shaker once it has dried and let your child thread yarn through the holes.

Ages Five to Seven (Transitional Kindergarten, Kindergarten, and Lower Elementary)

Easy Spiced Salt Dough

This "cooking" lesson will introduce your child to mathematical concepts like proportions and fractions if you show them how to measure out the ingredients. The recipe will make a tennis ball–size lump of dough. Please do not eat.

You will need:

½ cup flour

⅛ cup salt

¼ cup water for boiling

2 teaspoons cooking oil

¼ cup room-temperature water

Ground spices or herbs (cinnamon, ginger, allspice, pumpkin spice, rosemary, dill, turmeric, etc.)

Mix the flour and salt together in a bowl.

Boil ¼ cup water in a small non-stick pot. Stir in the oil.

Add the flour and salt mixture to the pot gradually, stirring vigorously. Use your spoon to mash the ingredients together if needed.

Turn off the burner, and add ¼ cup room-temperature water. Incorporate this into the dough.

When it is cool enough to handle, turn the dough onto your counter or a cutting board and knead it until all the ingredients are combined and it feels soft.

The dough will vary based on factors like humidity and type of flour used. If the dough is sticky, add more flour. If it is crumbly, add more water.

Let your child pick the spices to add. Start with ¼ teaspoon and knead in more if necessary.

Grass Heads

I did this project with a large group of students, and they loved it. I recommend this for any crafting get-togethers, like scout meetings or birthday parties. Grass seed is available in small amounts (for patching your lawn) for just a few bucks, and you can often collect secondhand nylons or buy them cheaply at any dollar store.

You will need:

Grass seed

Nylon panty hose

Potting soil

Scissors

Small container, such as a glass or small pot

Hot glue gun

Plastic "googly" eyes

Red, pink, or brown pipe cleaner (optional)

Water

Spray bottle

Sprinkle a small handful of grass seed inside the toe of the nylon. This is your "hair." Add potting soil, and pack it into a ball shape. This is the "head."

Tie a knot in the nylon as close as possible to the ball of soil. Cut off all but 3–4 inches.

Put the ball into a container where the majority of the ball sticks out of the top.

Use the hot glue gun to glue googly eyes to the ball and a piece of pipe cleaner for a mouth if you like.

Add some water to your container, so that the tail of the nylon can wick up the moisture. Make sure to also spray the top with the seeds on a regular basis to keep it moist.

In a few days, you should start to see some sprouts. Let them grow through the nylon until they are tall enough to give your head a "haircut."

Action Nature Art

Children of almost any age like this open-ended style of painting. For older children, you can pair it with a discussion about types of abstract art and the various techniques used to make it.

You will need:

Cardstock or watercolor paper

Cardboard box

Masking tape (optional)

3 or more colors of acrylic paint

Paper plate

Acorns, pinecones, washed and dried avocado or peach
pits, almonds or walnuts still in the shell, sycamore
balls, "spiky balls" from the liquidambar (sweetgum)
tree, and other similar items from nature

Paint brushes (optional)

Place the paper inside the box. You may want to use some
masking tape to hold it in place.

Squeeze a dollop of paint onto the paper plate.

Dip your acorn, pinecone, or whatever into the paint,
making sure it is at least halfway covered, or use the paint
brush to add the paint.

Set this on the center of the paper. Roll the box around so
that the paint makes patterns.

You can use each nature ingredient separately, or you can
put them on the tray at the same time with different colors of
paint and watch how they interact with each other.

Ages Eight to Ten
(Middle to Upper Elementary)

Sprout House Snack Shack

This is a popular STEM (science, technology, engineering, and
math) craft, but in this version, you will be sprouting edible
microgreens that you can eat! Chia seeds work great, but I have
also used radish, arugula, kale, broccoli, flax, and mustard seeds.
The greens will taste a lot like the vegetables they eventually
turn into: for example, radish and arugula have a "peppery"
flavor, while chia and kale are milder.

You will need:

   Quick-sprouting seeds from edible plants

   Bowl of water

   5 or more sponges (plain sponges—do not use ones with
     a rough scrubbing side)

   Toothpicks

   Scissors

   Spray bottle with water

   Plastic bag

Place your seeds in a bowl of water and allow them to sit overnight.

Rinse the sponges thoroughly. Squeeze out the excess water so that they are damp, not wet.

Build your house by using toothpicks to hold the sponges together. Place two sponges at a 90-degree angle to each other to make the roof, and then add two sides to the roof for the house. Finally, place a sponge at the bottom to act as the floor. This will use 5 sponges. If you have more, you can cut them up and make a front and back for the house or "hedges" on either side of the walls. Use the scissors to cut off any toothpicks sticking out.

Once your house is built and your seeds have soaked, spread the seed mixture on the roof and any other flat surfaces. Cover your house at night with the plastic bag to keep moisture in, and uncover it during the day to keep it from molding. Spray it generously with water several times daily—don't let the sponges dry out!

Once your seeds start to sprout, they are edible! You may want to let them grow a few inches to maximize your harvest. Eat them alone or put them on sandwiches, in salads, on pasta, and so on.

Herbal Mandala

I love how this craft turns out, because just like a kaleidoscope, no two projects will ever be the same. It's also a fun way to introduce geometry to your child.

You will need:

Leaves, herbs, flower petals, or a combination of these

Waxed paper

Scissors

Plate

Pen

Iron

Rag or press cloth

Pick some leaves, herbs, or flowers. Avoid plants with thick stems or veins. The thinner and more pliable they are, the better. Flower petals will add color.

Cut a square piece of waxed paper. Trace a circle on it with a plate. Draw lines through the circle and divide it into sections to help you organize your mandala.

Place your plant material onto the waxed paper within the circle. Help your child make a geometric design using the lines as a guide.

Heat your iron on a low setting. Lay your mandala on the rag or press cloth. Cut another piece of waxed paper the same size as the first and cover your mandala with it.

Iron the two pieces of waxed paper together, with the plant matter inside. Once you iron one side, you should flip it over and iron the other side.

Cut out your mandala along the circular line you traced. Hang it in the window like a suncatcher to display your design.

Ages Ten and Up (Upper Elementary)

Veggie Stamps

If you find that you have some potatoes or carrots on hand that are past their prime, don't throw them away! Instead, you can use them to make these fun stamps. There are sharp knives involved, so make sure to supervise your child and show them how to handle these tools correctly.

You will need:

> Stamping surface (see below)
>
> Potatoes or root vegetables (carrots, parsnips, turnips, rutabagas, etc.)
>
> Cutting board
>
> Permanent marker
>
> Small knife (paring, utility, pocketknife, etc.)
>
> Paper towels
>
> Acrylic paint
>
> Cotton balls

Start by deciding what you want to print your stamps on. Acrylic paint will adhere to most porous surfaces, such as paper, canvas, cloth, wood, and unfinished ceramic.

Cut your vegetable on the cutting board so that there is a flat area for you to carve your stamp on. Make sure the area is big enough for your design!

Draw your stamp onto the vegetable with the marker. You can do this freehand, use a stencil, or print an image and use that to make a template.

Use your knife to cut away large pieces from around the stamp, and then go back after and carve it with more precise cuts until you are happy with the way it looks.

Wipe off the excess marker on your stamp with the paper towels, and blot your stamp periodically if the vegetable releases moisture.

Add paint to your stamp with a cotton ball. Make a test print on a piece of scrap paper. When you get a feel for how much paint you need, stamp your image onto your desired surface.

Woodsy Masquerade Masks

Thick cardstock (a cereal box is perfect)

Large shoe

Pen

Scissors

Hot glue gun and glue

Cheap plastic sunglasses (most dollar stores have these)

Plants (see next page)

Paint (any kind)

Paint brush

Ribbon or fabric trim (optional)

Elastic cord (optional)

Fold your piece of cardstock in half. Trace around either the front half or the back half of the shoe, depending on the shape you want. Cut out the shape on the folded cardstock, and unfold it to reveal a mask. You can further trim the mask shape if you like, and make sure to cut eyeholes.

Pop out the lenses of the glasses and hot glue the mask to them where you want it to sit on the face.

Pick out the leaves, plants, or herbs that you want to use for this project. Try flower petals or sturdy herbs like bay, mint, or sage. Just about any leaf will work. These will only last a few days, so if you want more longevity, try corn husks; small, light twigs or grasses; moss; bark; and evergreen needles. Make sure that whatever you add to your mask is not too heavy.

Paint the mask. Choose a color similar to the plants you will be using to make the mask look fuller.

If you want to layer the plant material like scales, start from the edges (near the ears) and overlap each row, working toward the eye holes.

When your mask is almost covered, glue a layer or two of plant matter around the eyes, overlapping the other plants. You can then add ribbon or fabric trim around the eyes or edges of the mask to give it a more finished look.

If you followed the directions but the mask is still too heavy, attach a piece of elastic to either side of the mask that will go around the head and help hold it up.

Plant
Profiles

Plant Profiles

This section features spotlights on individual herbs, highlighting their cultivation, history, and culinary, crafting, and medicinal uses. Refer to the key below for each plant's sun and water needs, listed in a helpful at-a-glance table.

Key to Plant Needs	
Sun	
Shade	—
Partial shade	☼
Partial sun	☼ ☼
Full sun	☼ ☼ ☼
Water	
Water sparingly	💧
	💧 💧
Water frequently	💧 💧 💧

USDA Hardiness Zones

The United States is organized into zones according to the average lowest annual winter temperature, indicating a threshold for cold tolerance in the area. This USDA Plant Hardiness Zone Map uses the latest available data. For best results, plant herbs that can withstand the climate of their hardiness zone(s) and bring less hardy plants indoors during colder weather. Seek additional resources for high summer temperatures, as these can vary within zones.

It is helpful to keep track of temperatures and frost dates in your neighborhood or check with a local gardening center or university extension for the most up-to-date record. Climate change and local topography will also affect your growing space, so compensate accordingly.

USDA Plant Hardiness Zone Map

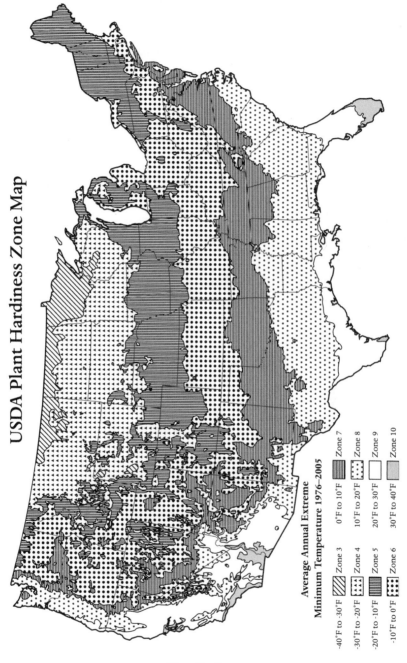

Average Annual Extreme Minimum Temperature 1976–2005

- -40°F to -30°F — Zone 3
- -30°F to -20°F — Zone 4
- -20°F to -10°F — Zone 5
- -10°F to 0°F — Zone 6
- 0°F to 10°F — Zone 7
- 10°F to 20°F — Zone 8
- 20°F to 30°F — Zone 9
- 30°F to 40°F — Zone 10

USDA Plant Hardiness Zone Map (Cont.)

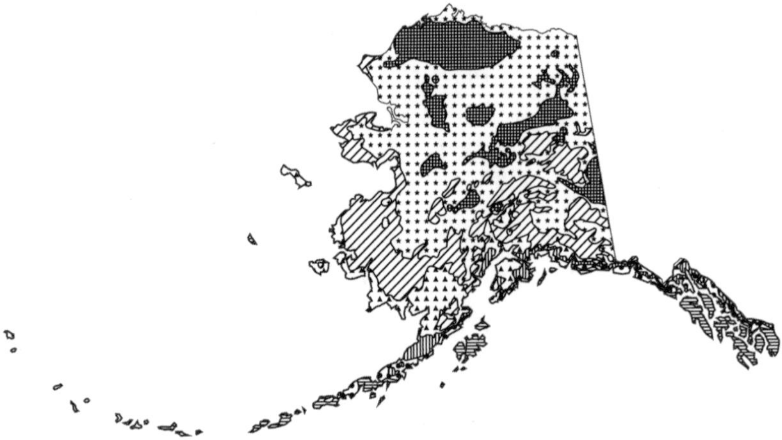

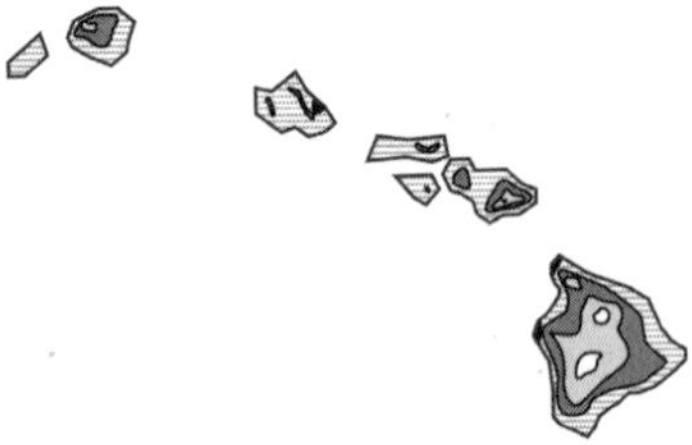

Average Annual Extreme
Minimum Temperature 1976–2005

-60°F to -50°F	Zone 1
-50°F to -40°F	Zone 2
-40°F to -30°F	Zone 3
-30°F to -20°F	Zone 4
-20°F to -10°F	Zone 5
-10°F to 0°F	Zone 6
0°F to 10°F	Zone 7
10°F to 20°F	Zone 8
20°F to 30°F	Zone 9
30°F to 40°F	Zone 10
40°F to 50°F	Zone 11
50°F to 60°F	Zone 12
60°F to 70°F	Zone 13

Marjoram

❧ Anne Sala ❧

If you decide to plant marjoram in your garden, be sure to mark its location well. It is easy to confuse it with other herbs. But don't feel bad if you do; people have been misidentifying it for thousands of years.

A tender, sweetly scented herb, marjoram is part of the expansive mint family, Lamiaceae. Its scientific name *Origanum* is Greek for "joy of the mountain" and refers to marjoram's native mountain habitat in the Mediterranean and Eurasia. Marjoram is closely related to the more familiar cooking herb, oregano. In fact, throughout the ages, the names *marjoram* and *oregano* have sometimes been used interchangeably—much to the consternation of later herbalists, including me!

Marjoram	
Species	*Origanum majorana*
Zone	9–10
Needs	☀☀☀ 💧
Soil pH	5.5–6.5
Size	1–2 ft. tall

Origanum majorana is considered to be "true" marjoram, and is commonly called "sweet marjoram." There is also *Origanum onites*, or pot marjoram, and *Origanum dictamnus*, or dittany of Crete. In an attempt to cut down confusion, I focus on the uses of sweet marjoram in this article.

Sweet marjoram can grow up to two feet high with vertical stems sporting small, gray-green, oval leaves covered in soft hairs. In mid to late summer, it will send up stalks that hold white flowers. These flowers mature into little capsules that hold four seeds, or "nutlets." Another name for sweet marjoram is "knotted marjoram," which is a reference to the way its flowers are uniquely clustered. No matter how the flowers look, pollinators love them.

It is difficult to describe marjoram without comparing it to oregano (*Origanum vulgare*). When sniffed side by side, marjoram has a spicy scent that ends on a delicate, lemony note. Oregano's spicy scent ends on a robust, peppery note.

Growing Marjoram

As a family, oreganos are a hardy bunch of perennials, but not sweet marjoram. In most areas of the world, it is treated as an annual and can be quite picky about its growing conditions. To grow your own, I suggest starting seeds in a pot or seed tray before planting them in the ground since the seeds are quite small. Give marjoram sandy soil that drains quickly. Spread the seeds over the top of the soil and cover them with a light sprinkling of more soil or vermiculite. Water regularly though sparingly as the seeds come up, which can take between five days and a month, depending on the temperature of the soil—the warmer the better.

The seedlings are susceptible to rot in their first weeks, so don't get too attached just yet. Pull out any that look like they aren't going to make it. Once the plants have a few true leaves, you can move them to their permanent spots. If that is in the ground, make sure it is well past the last frost of spring.

"About [Hymen's] temples bind the bloom,
Of Marjoram flow'ret scented sweet;
Take flamey veil: glad hither come
Come hither borne by snow-hue'd feet
Wearing the saffron'd sock."
—Gaius Valerius Catullus (c. 84–c. 54 BCE),
"Epithalamium on Vinia and Manlius"

When I first tried to grow marjoram from seed, I planted wild thyme at the same time in an identical pot. I forgot to mark them and after waiting ages for the seeds to sprout, I could no longer remember which seeds were in which pot. A week or so later, it suddenly became easy to tell the difference— my marjoram sprouts were the dead ones! That wild thyme, however, was the happiest plant I have ever grown.

Once established, marjoram is a pretty plant that loves the sun. Snipping its stems encourages new growth, so use its leaves in food, tea, bouquets—everything!

History and Lore

Marjoram's history is entwined with nearly every ritual of life surrounding the Mediterranean. Its leaves have been found on mummies in Egypt, where the herb was called *sopho* and it was sacred to the crocodile-headed god, Sobek. Across the sea in Greece and Rome, if marjoram was found growing by the grave of a loved one, it meant they were happy in the afterlife. The herb was considered to be sacred to the goddess of love— Aphrodite in Greece and Venus in Rome—where myth has it that Venus gave marjoram its scent "to remind mortals of her beauty," write Belsinger and Dille in *Cooking with Herbs*.

In honor of the goddesses of love, brides and grooms wore crowns of marjoram at their wedding. Today, women and girls in the Ukraine and India continue to adorn themselves with marjoram. In the Ukraine, marjoram is woven into simple head wreaths as well elaborate headdresses as a symbol of maternal love. In India, marjoram is wound with jasmine blossoms into fragrant hair garlands.

Marjoram is an important component in a variety of folk-loric applications. Marjoram could make a woman dream of her future husband if she slept with it under her pillow, and it could ward away evil and spells if grown by the front door. If you kept it on your person, it would attract wealth.

In the medical world, marjoram was used for a multitude of ailments. It could be used to extract splinters as well as to counteract poison. Last, marjoram was (and still is) valued for its antibacterial properties and is often used to treat skin conditions.

Marjoram and Jasmine Green Tea Dry Shampoo

In India, marjoram is not typically used in food, but it is available in flower shops because, like I wrote above, it is a popular herb to combine with jasmine flowers in garlands. I was curious to experience this scent combination myself and thought a dry shampoo would be a fun way to do it. I am writing this

article during the COVID-19 pandemic and my ability to h.
for ingredients is limited. That is why the jasmine fragrance i
coming by way of a scented green tea. As a bonus, green tea is
beneficial for the hair and scalp as well.

Dry shampoos seem like a beauty aid from a bygone era,
but they never really went away. One can even purchase commercially made dry shampoos today. Bloggers tout them as a
must-have for on-the-go days when there's no time for a traditional shower. I wouldn't go so far as to say that, myself—I
feel like I just traded fifteen minutes in the shower for fifteen
minutes of hair care—but dry shampoos are convenient when
camping or you are waiting for a plumber to come fix a leaky
bathtub (true story!).

Dry shampoos work because the powder absorbs oily
buildup in your hair. Then, when you brush the powder out,
it takes the oils, dirt, and other styling products with it. After-
ward, you are left with soft, aromatic hair that is full of body.

There are lots of ingredients that can be used to create dry
shampoos, such as cornstarch, cornmeal, rice flour, clay, and
salt. I came across several recipes calling for baking soda, but it
can cause skin irritation and may actually be harmful to your
hair, so I don't recommend using it. If you have darker hair or
red hair, switch out 1–2 tablespoons of cornstarch in the recipe below for unsweetened cocoa powder, espresso powder, or
cinnamon. It will change the scent of the shampoo, but it will
be less "dusty" looking in your hair.

This recipe makes about ½ cup.

Tools

Electric spice grinder

Plastic or glass container with lid (make sure they are
completely dry)

makeup brush or paint brush

airbrush

ents

2 tablespoons uncooked white rice, divided

2 tablespoons dried marjoram leaves

2 sachets or 2 teaspoons jasmine-scented green tea

¼ cup cornstarch

Measure out 1 tablespoon of rice and put it into the electric spice grinder. Add the marjoram leaves and grind until the contents become a fine powder. Carefully pour the contents into your container.

Measure out the other tablespoon of rice into the grinder. Add the tea and grind it into fine powder, then pour it into your container.

Add the cornstarch to the container and close the lid securely. Shake the powders to combine them.

When applying, you must first be sure your hair is completely dry; otherwise, the powder will become a sticky glue. Also, you must (*ahem*) use this on hair that has not been washed recently. Last, find a good location in or around your home to apply the shampoo. I suggest doing it while leaning over a bathroom sink or even outdoors.

Take the makeup brush and dip the tips of the bristles into the powder. Tap off any excess then dab the brush along your part and hairline before working the brush back into the rest of your hair. If you are doing this in front of a mirror, don't let the white residue alarm you—you are going to brush it all out in a little bit. If you have long hair, lift the hair in sections and dab at the roots. While still leaning forward, run your fingers through your hair and search for spots that still feel oily.

Let the powder sit in your hair for about 10 minutes, then vigorously brush it out. Again, do this over your sink, in the bathtub or shower, or outside. After you are done, rinse your hairbrush in cold water to remove the powder.

Marjoram's Culinary Contributions

A 2002 study called *Oregano: The genera Origanum and Lippia* claimed *Origanum vulgare* (the type of oregano you taste in your pizza sauce) is the most popular culinary herb in the world. Marjoram, however, has nearly been forgotten in the United States. In the seventeenth and eighteenth centuries, colonists brought it over with them from England, where it had been used since at least the thirteenth century to flavor desserts and as a salad ingredient. Before that, it is speculated that marjoram was introduced to the rest of continental Europe by the Roman Empire as it made its push throughout the land.

Like oregano, marjoram pairs well with tomatoes, all meats, and eggs. What I find intriguing is marjoram's affinity for fruit, custards, and seafood. I don't think oregano is as good at doing that.

I grew up in a home that did not use marjoram—or oregano, for that matter. My father is allergic to all members of *Origanum*, so I did not start experimenting with their flavors until I was living on my own. Even so, marjoram rarely made it into my shopping basket, and I feel bad about that now. I have been missing out on a truly special gift from the herb world.

The national cuisines around the Mediterranean still favor marjoram for its unique qualities, as well as Polish and

German, in which it flavors soups and certain varieties of sausage.

Kielbasa and Leek Soup

I have been making this soup for fifteen years, but I always used dry oregano. By swapping in fresh sweet marjoram, it is a completely different soup! The oregano version needed beer to pair with it. The marjoram one pairs with white wine.

- 2–3 medium leeks, halved lengthwise then chopped, dark green parts discarded
- 1 whole kielbasa sliced into thin half-moon shapes
- 1 tablespoon extra-virgin olive oil
- 2 large carrots, diced small
- 1 rib celery, diced small
- 8 cups low-sodium chicken stock
- 5 tablespoons flour
- 3 medium Yukon Gold potatoes, peeled and diced into ½-inch pieces
- 2 tablespoons chopped fresh marjoram, divided
- Salt and pepper to taste

Fill a large bowl with cold water and dump in the chopped leeks. Swish them around to remove any grit caught between the layers. Change the water if necessary.

While the leeks soak, place a wide-bottomed dutch oven or heavy pot over medium heat. Lightly brown the kielbasa slices and remove to a plate.

Add the olive oil to the pot and saute the carrots and celery until softened. Drain the leeks and add them to the carrots and celery. Cook until they are softened as well.

Add the stock, raise the heat to high and bring to a boil. After about 1 minute, reduce the heat and simmer partially covered for 15 minutes.

While the soup is simmering, place flour in a small bowl and carefully stir in small increments of hot broth to make a roux. Continue until the roux is smooth, then pour into the pot and stir.

When the soup returns to a simmer, add the kielbasa, potatoes, 1 tablespoon marjoram, salt, and pepper. Raise the heat to bring everything to a boil, then reduce the heat again. Allow it to simmer until the potatoes are cooked, about 10 minutes.

Just before serving, stir in the final tablespoon of marjoram. Ladle into wide bowls and round out the meal with bread and a crisp salad. Serves 6.

Za'atar

Growing in the mountains of several Middle Eastern countries is another marjoram relative: *Origanum syriacum*, or *za'atar*. It is said to have the scent and flavor of oregano, marjoram, and thyme combined into one. It is often used in a spice blend called za'atar, which also includes sumac and sesame seeds. It is a common seasoning found throughout the region, and every country and household has their own special way of making it. You can sprinkle it on bread, Greek yogurt, or roasted vegetables. You can even use it in a marinade for meat.

Za'atar is proving difficult to grow on a commercial scale outside of its native habitat even as this ingredient gains popularity. Cooks in other parts of the world are experimenting with za'atar's cousins to create an acceptable substitute blend.

I prefer the way sweet marjoram—rather than oregano—pairs with the other ingredients.

1 tablespoon sesame seeds

¼ cup dried thyme leaves

1 tablespoon dried marjoram leaves

2 teaspoons ground sumac or lemon zest

1 teaspoon salt

In a small pan over medium low heat, toast the sesame seeds for 1–2 minutes. Shake the pan or stir constantly—the seeds can scorch quickly.

While the seeds cool, grind the thyme and marjoram with a mortar and pestle. You aren't trying to make a powder; you're just trying to break some of the leaves down.

Add the sesame seeds and lightly crush them.

Pour the contents into an airtight container. Add the sumac or lemon zest and salt. Stir to combine. This recipe makes almost ½ cup.

A simple way to use this is to grill chicken with it: combine half of your za'atar with the juice of 1 lemon, 2 minced garlic cloves, 1–2 tablespoons of olive oil, and more salt. Coat your chicken pieces in it and marinate for at least 30 minutes and up to 4 hours. Cook on a hot grill and serve on a bed of bitter greens with lemon wedges.

⁓

Our modern tastebuds have been trained to crave big flavors—high fat, lots of salt, eye-wateringly hot. Marjoram can't compete with that. But in the end, we are the ones who lose because marjoram provides a taste that is unique in today's flavor palate. And new tastes are what I think we crave most of all. So the next time you see sweet marjoram for sale at your garden shop or in the grocery store, toss it in your cart and get ready to discover a forgotten realm of flavors.

Resources

Belsinger, Susan, and Carolyn Dille. *Cooking with Herbs.* New York: Van Nostrand Reinhold, 1984. Page 113.

Catullus, Gaius Valerius. *Carmina.* Edited by Richard Francis Burton. London, 1984. Electronic transcription by Perseus Digital Library. Poem 61, lines 6–10. http://perseus.uchicago.edu/perseus-cgi /citequery3.pl?dbname=PerseusLatinTexts&query=Catul.%20 61&getid=1.

Cox, Janice. "DIY Dry Shampoos." *Herb Quarterly,* fall 2014.

Hartung, Tammi. *Homegrown Herbs: A Complete Guide to Growing, Using, and Enjoying More Than 100 Herbs.* North Adams, MA: Storey Publishing, 2011.

Henry, Diana. *A Bird in the Hand: Chicken Recipes for Every Day and Every Mood.* New York: Hachette, 2015.

Hollis, Sarah. *The Country Diary Herbal.* New York: Henry Holt and Company, 1990.

Kintzios, Spiridon E., ed. *Oregano: The genera Origanum and Lippia.* London: Taylor & Francis, 2002.

Metzger, Christine. *Culinaria Germany: A Celebration of Food and Tradition.* Germany: h.f.ullmann publishing GmbH, 1999.

Meyers, Michelle. *Oregano and Marjoram: An Herb Society of America Guide to the Genus Origanum.* Kirtland, OH: The Herb Society of America, 2005. https://www.herbsociety.org/file_download /inline/b30630e2-d0a9-4632-a7da-14af53a07a67.

Schlosser, Katherine. *The Herb Society of America's Essential Guide to Growing and Cooking with Herbs.* Baton Rouge: Louisiana State University Press, 2007.

Venkateshwaran, Ramya. "6 Top Benefits & Uses of Marjoram for Health, Skin & Hair (*Sweet marjoram | Origanum majorana*)." *Wild Turmeric* (blog), January 29, 2015. https://www.wildturmeric.net /top-6-health-benefits-uses-of-marjoram-for-health-skin-hair/.

Red Clover

⤷ Rachael Witt ⤶

Reaching toward the sky, red clover grows larger than any true clover and extends a welcoming bloom in an array of places. From farm fields to restoration sites, forest edges to roadsides, and companion-planted gardens to herbal apothecaries, this plant offers diverse uses.

Red clover is a widespread, naturalized plant from Eurasia that is now found at low to mid elevations throughout the United States. Depending on where you're located, red clover is either referred to as a short-lived perennial, a biennial, or a self-seeding annual. This herbaceous plant will grow in heavy clay soils as well as sandy-loamy substrate.

Red clover can further be identified by its Latin name, *Trifolium pratense.*

Red Clover	
Species	*Trifolium pratense*
Zone	4–9
Needs	☼☼☼ 💧💧
Soil pH	6.0–6.5
Size	18–30 in. tall

Trifolium denotes that its leaves have three parts (known as leaflets). *Pratense* is said to be of a meadow. It dwells in pastures, fields, meadows, roadsides, and places of disturbance. Distinguishably different from other clovers, red clover bears a white V-shaped marking at the base of each leaflet. The soft, finely haired leaflets alternately grow along the stem, extending up to 30 inches in height.

From early to late summer, red clover is easily identified by its densely clustered pink-purple flower heads nestled on top of a pair of leaflets. What appears to be one flower is actually an inflorescence of twenty to 400 florets. At the base of each floret lies a drop of nectar providing sweetness for honey bees, pollinators, and humans too!

Once the flowers begin to show off their bright fuchsia-colored inflorescence, I begin to harvest. With bare hands, I pick the flowering tops by pinching the stem underneath the pair of leaflets at the base of the flower head. Be sure to gather red clover while it is in its freshest state. Avoid flowers beginning to turn brown, for the flowering head is known to quickly die back on the plant.

Red Clover in the Garden

Traditionally, red clover was planted after a corn crop to help restore fertility in the soil. Hence, it was referred to as "mother of the corn." Red clover sends down sturdy roots deep into the earth to help break up compacted and clay-rich soils. As a member of the pea family, Fabaceae, it embodies the role of a nitrogen-fixing legume that nourishes the soil. Farmers will use red clover seed as a cover crop to restore soils or as livestock feed.

Whether you're growing hay or herbs, oat straw and red clover make a great combination for companion planting. An early harvest of oats in their milky oat state will optimize water and light for red clover to bloom and be harvested thereafter. Small-clumps of red clover can also be planted as a companion in the garden. I encourage red clover to flourish among my low-growing culinary herbs for an extra pop to the greenery. It makes for a beautiful sight when this plant grows in between sage and oregano or even kale and chard!

To best cultivate red clover, disperse seeds among rich, well-drained soil in full sun to partial shade. After the last frost in spring, I broadcast seeds over a well-prepared garden bed, raking them in no deeper than a quarter inch in depth. Red clover seed can be sown in the fall (ideally one month prior to the average first frost) or earlier in the spring for more temperate zones. The earlier the seed is planted, the more opportunity for a greater yield over the growing season.

Red Clover in the Kitchen

Red clover is an edible flower that is fresh and subtly sweet. The flowering tops are rich in vitamins B and C, calcium, chromium, magnesium, nickel, potassium, and phosphorus. Due to its richness in vitamins, minerals, and phytonutrients, red clover is nourishing food as medicine.

Sweet Summer Salad

One of my favorite ways to enjoy red clover is by picking apart the individual florets and enjoying their taste of nectar. To share my delight with others, I like to sprinkle the florets on top of salads.

For the salad:
- 1 small head lettuce, torn apart
- 1 large handful dandelion greens, torn apart
- 1 bunch spinach, shredded
- ¼ cup clover sprouts (or any sprouts available)
- ¼ cup raspberries, sliced or whole
- ½ cup red clover blossoms, separated
- ½ cup calendula blossoms, petals separated
- 2 tablespoons lavender blossoms, separated
- ½ cup crumbled feta cheese, optional

For the dressing:
- ⅓ cup red wine vinegar
- 1 cup oil
- 1 tablespoon dijon mustard
- 2 tablespoons honey
- 1 teasoon salt
- ¼ teasoon black pepper

Place the greens in a bowl. Top with sprouts, raspberries, separated flower petals, and feta cheese, if desired. In a separate bowl, combine vinegar, oil, mustard, and honey. Add salt and pepper. Pour dressing onto salad, and toss before serving. Serves 4.

Lady Love Oxymel

If we are going to take herbs internally, they might as well taste good! This combination of herbs, vinegar, and honey almost immediately has my mouth salivating and my heart at ease. The following herbs support our circulatory system, nourish our bones, strengthen our immune system, and provide sweetness for our heart and spleen.

An oxymel is a honey-vinegar infusion. Traditionally used as an electrolyte, oxymels help wake up your digestive enzymes while boosting your energy and immunity. I take 1 tablespoon in the morning or add to carbonated water for an afternoon pick-me-up.

1 cup fresh hawthorn berries

½ cup fresh rose hips

½ cup chopped red clover flowering tops, fresh or dried

¼ cup chopped motherwort aerial parts, fresh or dried

Quart jar

1–2 cardamom pods, dried and crushed

2–3 cups red wine vinegar

2–3 cups raw honey

Add hawthorn fruit, rose hips, red clover, and motherwort to a quart jar. Crush cardamom pods and add to the jar. Pour vinegar over the herbs until half the jar is half full. Fill the rest of the jar with honey, leaving room to stir. Stir to release any air bubbles and combine honey, vinegar, and herbs. Add a splash of vinegar to top off the oxymel to the brim of the jar. Cover with a non-corrosive lid (plastic wrap topped with a metal lid works well or a BPA-free plastic jar lid). Store in room temperature and out of direct light. Shake daily for 2 weeks. Infuse up to 4 weeks, then taste for potency.

When the infusion is ready, strain out the herbs. Pour decanted oxymel into a flip-top jar or glass jar with non-corrosive lid. Keep in a cool place in the kitchen or refrigerate. Keeps for 1 year.

this oxymel as a morning tonic, add it to drinks, or
ne it with oils for a salad dressing.

Red Clover in the Apothecary

Red clover is used fresh or completely dried for herbal preparations. I tend toward making teas and infusions with red
clover because I get to fully experience the flavor of the herb
while also absorbing the phytonutrients that might otherwise
be destroyed in an alcohol-based tincture. When needed, I
make a small batch of fresh red clover tincture. Most often,
I dry the rest of my harvest to store for tea combinations, infusions, or external poultices and baths.

Red clover is revered for its gentle yet effective healing
properties. Most notably, red clover is a traditional liver and
blood tonic, a women's hormone ally, and a mild antispasmodic for coughs.

Red clover is cooling, bitter, and slightly sweet. According
to Traditional Chinese Medicine, red clover clears heat, resolves
fire toxicity, and quickens blood. "Toxic heat" or "heat in the
blood" can be seen as swelling and inflammation, infections,
skin rashes, and congested lymphatic glands. Ailments such as
arthritis, tumors, skin eruptions, and lung congestion can be
relieved with red clover—and overall, it is most effective when
combined with other herbs that are specific to the ailments.
For example, native herbs such as angelica, elecampane, white
pine, and false Solomon's seal used in combination with
red clover traditionally treated bronchial problems and sore
throats and helped further expectorate.

In Western herbalism, red clover is called an **alterative**.
It helps the body eliminate metabolic wastes, further cleans-
ing toxins from our lymphatic system and nourishing our

liver and kidneys. In both herbal traditions, red clover is used for skin rashes such as eczema, psoriasis, and acne, as well as supporting the lymphatic system to clear swollen, congested glands and lymph nodes. To reduce eczema outbreaks and irritations, I make a tincture with red clover, Oregon grape root, burdock, cleavers, chickweed, dandelion, and nettles. Red clover contains blood-thinning coumarins, so it's advised to not use red clover when taking blood-thinning medications nor use it during pregnancy.

Red clover is an esteemed phytoestrogen herb. Women have used red clover to improve fertility, relieve chronic painful menstruation, harmonize uneven menstrual cycles, and reduce hot flashes while nourishing and strengthening bone health during perimenopause and menopause. Red clover has such a high vitamin, mineral, and protein content that it helps restore and balance hormonal functions. It is an alkaline herb that imparts calmness on the nervous system and promotes fertility. In recent years, red clover's estrogenic isoflavone compounds have arguably been of concern for increasing cancer recurrence in estrogen-receptor positive cancer. On the contrary, it is also valued for antitumor compounds that can help as a cancer preventative, especially breast and female reproductive cancer. Until further research is published, it's advised to use caution with red clover in cases of estrogen-receptor positive cancer.

Red Clover Infusion

An infusion of the flowers is one of the best ways to obtain red clover's nutritious and medicinal potency. Red clover's gentle action is helpful for both children and the elderly and can be used for long-term consumption. I make a red clover infusion on a weekly basis and drink 1 quart of the infusion over the course of 1–2 days.

1 ounce dried red clover flowering tops

1 tablespoon dried peppermint, optional for a "fertility brew"

1 quart boiling water

Place the dried herb in a quart jar. Fill the jar to the top with boiling water. Stir the herb to allow for air bubbles to escape. Secure the lid on top of the jar. Infuse for 4 hours or overnight. Strain the herb from infusion by pouring over a strainer into another jar or bowl. Drink at least 8 ounces of infusion per day. Store in the refrigerator for up to 3 days.

Drying Red Clover

It is important to thoroughly dry red clover. Research has found that wilted blossoms can create a potent anticoagulant called dicoumarol. It is also one of the more difficult plants to properly dry. Red clover is prone to fermenting or quickly composting in its flower form. To maintain good quality dried herb, make sure to dry the flowering tops thoroughly and carefully.

- Place herbs in single layer on drying racks or a flat basket or screen.

- For baskets and screens, place in a dry environment with plenty of airflow.

- If using a dehydrator, place the rack in the dehydrator at 95 to 100 degrees Fahrenheit.

- Turn flowers over frequently.

- Store once all moisture is removed and flowers are brittle.

——◦——

Red clover represents healing and good health. It's a plant that provides nutrients for the soil, nectar for pollinators, food for grazers, beauty for onlookers, vitamins and minerals for our meals, and gentle medicine for our bodies. Red clover is an indicator of hope for biodiversity.

Resources

Alfs, Matthew. *300 Herbs: Their Indications & Contraindications*. New Brighton, MN: Old Theology Book House, 2003. Page 91.

Garran, Thomas Avery. *Western Herbs According to Traditional Chinese Medicine: A Practitioner's Guide*. Rochester, VT: Healing Arts Press, 2008.

"How to Grow Red Clover: Guide to Growing Red Clover." Heirloom Organics. Accessed Deember 4, 2020. http://www.heirloom-organics.com/guide/va/1/guidetogrowingredclover.html.

Kloos, Scott. *Pacific Northwest Medicinal Plants: Identify, Harvest, and Use 120 Wild Herbs for Health and Wellness*. Portland, OR: Timber Press, 2017.

Moore, Michael. *Medicinal Plants of the Mountain West*. Rev. ed. Santa Fe: Museum of New Mexico Press, 1979.

Phillips, Roger. *Wild Food*. London: Pan Macmillan, 2014.

Tierra, Michael. *The Way of Herbs*. New York: Simon and Schuster, 1998.

Tilgner, Sharol Marie. *Herbal Medicine from the Heart of the Earth*. 2nd ed. Pleasant Hill, OR: Wise Acres, 2009.

Weed, Susun S. *Menopausal Years: The Wise Woman Way*. Woodstock, NY: Ash Tree Publishing, 1992.

———. *Wise Woman Herbal for the Childbearing Year*. Woodstock, NY: Ash Tree Publishing, 1986.

Hydrangea

☙ JD Hortwort ❧

Anyone looking for a plant that can provide interest over the bulk of the year should look no further than the hydrangea family of plants. While the plant is deciduous, when it does start to grow as the weather warms up, it goes full bore. The leaves are broad, and the flower heads are striking and come in a variety of shapes. In addition, if you get the right kind, the color display goes on well into fall.

Fresh or dried, just a few hydrangea flowers fill a vase or basket. Once dried, you can make a lusciously full wreath for the door or wall using only hydrangea blossoms. However, these flowers mix so well with other plants that you can come up with

Hydrangea	
Species	*Hydrangea* spp.
Zone	3–9
Needs	☼☼ ◐ ◐
Soil pH	5.5–7
Size	6 × 6 ft., mature

endless combinations using strawflowers, nandina (and other berries), eucalyptus stems, cotton bolls, dried roses, burlap or gingham ribbons, and so many other materials.

The large flower heads make instant, grand statements, but you can also break these big bloomers up. My sister once used smaller clusters of the individual flowers to decorate a Victorian Christmas tree. The muted tones of dried hydrangeas are lovely, but the flower also takes very nicely to light sprays of gold, silver, bronze, or copper paint. Pick out and flatten single flowers to glue onto homemade greeting and friendship cards.

But before you start any craft projects, the catch (and isn't there always a catch?) is to get the right kind of snowball bush. In fact, not only do you have to get the right kind of hydrangea, you have to make sure the plant you purchase is truly a hydrangea and not a viburnum.

Know Your Snowballs

Hydrangea and viburnum can look a lot alike, especially if you are standing in a nursery looking at a plant tag that reads "snowball bush." Despite appearances, these two plants aren't even kissing cousins. Hydrangea belongs to the plant family Hydrangeaceae; viburnum, to the plant family Adoxaceae.

It's an easy mistake to make. In my family, we grew up calling just about every shrub with big, rounded white flower clusters "snowball bushes." My sisters and I adored Grandma's big bush that sat at the edge of the garden, right outside her kitchen window. We each vowed to have one just like it when we set up housekeeping. The problem was, we keep coming up with *Hydrangea arborescens*, the snowball bush that is native to the United States, and wondering why it just didn't look quite like Grandma's.

We eventually learned it was because Grandma had *Viburnum macrocephalum*, the Chinese snowball bush. Grandma was no help in the matter. She could grow just about anything, but once she had a plant in the ground and well established, she was on to other things. Grandma wasn't inclined to keep plant tags or a gardening journal. In fact, she probably rooted a cutting of her snowball bush from a friend or relative. Garden centers and nurseries were few and far between back in the day. If you didn't root your own, get one from a friend, or order it from a garden catalog, that plant was just a pretty picture in a magazine.

So how do you make sure you get a hydrangea? The easiest thing to do is read the fine print on the plant tag and make sure it reads *Hydrangea*. If you have inherited one because it came with the house you purchased or currently rent, you'll have to do a little sleuthing.

One quick and easy tell is to determine the plant hardiness zone you live in. The United States is divided into 13 zones that indicate the average coldest winter temperature in the zone. For example, North Carolina has three zones where the cold temperatures in winter can range between minus 15 degrees Fahrenheit to 20 degrees above zero.

Since the Chinese snowball bush can't survive the winters above zone 6, if you live in zone 5 and above, you probably have an old-fashioned hydrangea snowball bush.

Next, check the height of the bush. If it is taller than six feet, it is probably a viburnum. These shrubs range between six and ten feet tall at maturity, while hydrangeas stay usually below six feet tall.

Finally, take a close look at the flower head. Both snowball hydrangea and viburnum flowers start out pea-green and mature to white. While hydrangea flower heads are large, viburnum flower clusters are monsters by comparison. You can also note the timing of the bloom. Hydrangea will start to form a flower earlier than viburnum.

Beyond Snowballs

Today, you can get snowball hydrangea in a variety of colors. But you don't have to limit yourself to snowballs.

Mopheads

Many people think of the blue-flowering French hydrangea (*H. macrophylla*) when hydrangeas are mentioned. This is also the one that gardeners talk about when they discuss adding lime to the planting soil to change the color of the flower from blue to pink. French hydrangeas are sensitive to the acidity of the soil they are planted in. This is a reference to the pH of the soil. When the soil pH is 6 or lower, the flower is blue. Adding lime to the soil will raise the pH or, in gardening parlance, "sweeten" the soil. In alkaline soils, *H. arborescens* blooms pink. When 'Nikko Blue' (*H. macrophylla* 'Nikko Blue') was all we had to work with in the garden, adjusting the soil pH was the only way to get that pink color. Hybridizers have had a field day in the past couple of decades, coming up with French hydrangea that will stay reliably pink (or cherry or rose) without playing around with soil amendments.

Lacecaps (*H. macrophylla* var. *normalis*) and mountain hydrangeas (*H. macrophylla* ssp. *serrata*) also fall in the mophead category. The flatter bloom cluster of a lacecap has large flowers around the edge and tiny buds in the middle as if not all the flowers ever got around to opening. The buds in the center are fertile; the larger blooms on the edge are sterile. Lacecaps are available in colors ranging from white to pink to blue and purple. Mountain hydrangea looks a lot like lacecap but with smaller flowers and like its cousin, comes in a variety of colors.

No blooming shrub makes a statement in the landscape quite like the hydrangea. In addition to providing beautiful floral displays, it is the easiest flower in the garden to use for craft projects that will last throughout the year.

Oakleafs

Oakleaf hydrangeas (*H. quercifolia*) get their name from their broad leaves that bear a resemblance to certain types of oak foliage. The flowers are conical-shaped showstoppers that start out white, become tinged with pink and fade to a soft tan. The foliage is nothing to sneeze at either, adding tones of russet, bronze, and purple to the fall landscape.

Panicle

Peegee or panicled hydrangeas (*H. paniculata*) are an exception to the rule about height for this category of plants. Peegees can get over fifteen feet tall with just a little encouragement. In fact, some people train them up into small trees just like crepe myrtles. The flowers are long, white cones, longer than those of the oakleaf hydrangea, and tinged with pink. As the plant matures, the tan and burgundy bark exfoliates or shreds, adding an element of interest in the winter landscape.

Vining

Vining or climbing hydrangeas (*H. anomala*) are probably less well known compared to their bushy cousins. The Japanese climbing hydrangea has a white flower similar to a lacecap although much smaller. While it will eventually grow to about twenty-five to thirty feet long, it will do so in a very slow and deliberate manner, in my experience. Its Chinese cousin, *H. anomala* ssp. *petiolaris*, will run faster and farther, over seventy feet.

Planting Guidelines

Regardless of the type of hydrangea you pick for your landscape, it needs well-drained, well-amended soil. In the first year after planting, be sure your hydrangea doesn't dry out but don't let the soil stay too wet, either. Hydrangeas don't have a lot of pests or disease problems but a susceptibility to root rot is one of them.

This plant grows best in a partially shaded location, making it a perfect addition to woodland settings that have high, dappled shade. One tip is the farther south you go, the more shade the plant will require. Below zone 7, I would not install a hydrangea in a southern or western location that gets full sun all day long.

Once established, hydrangeas don't need a lot of fertilizer. Providing a general purpose fertilizer once a year in the spring is usually sufficient.

Pruning

Here's a question that comes up, year after year. When do I prune my hydrangea?

Mopheads are pruned just after bloom because they tend to set next year's flowers on this year's wood. Unless you have one of the new ever-blooming varieties, in which case, you can thin the stems at any time to keep the bush tidy.

Oakleaf hydrangea is also pruned just after flowering, unless you are saving the flowers to dry naturally on the shrub either for fall displays or indoor dried flower arrangements. In that case, you don't prune much at all but allow the shrub to grow in its loose natural shape, thinning out the oldest stems each season.

Then, there are the Peegee and those native snowball bushes which bloom on new wood, so you can cut them back in later winter or early spring. Vining hydrangeas are rarely pruned except to train or control the vine.

If this all sounds too confusing, what should you do? The easiest thing to do is prune any flowering shrub shortly after it flowers. Limit your cuts to removing the old, dead, or non-productive wood.

Or just chuck the pruners all together and let your hydrangea do its thing. You can limit your pruning to simply snipping off the flowers at the end of the season. Hydrangeas grow informally but not in a messy habit. They are a bit like loose, fluffy green clouds with the added bonus of beautiful, fluffy flowers! Why mess with perfection?

❧ Plant Profiles ❧

Yerba Maté

⤜ Sally Cragin ⤛

Coffee or tea? Tea or coffee? Dwellers of the West have been asking that question for centuries with pleasure. Starting your day with a caffeinated beverage has been a huge motivator for many of us in the writing profession. When I think of the newsrooms I've worked in, it was the rare journalist who didn't have a battle-stained ceramic coffee cup (or several) taking pride of place next to the pencil jar and desk phone.

Some years back, I scaled back my full-octane coffee drinking and began exploring the wild world of tea—black, green, white, floral, citrus, herbal, and more. This is even more fun with clear glass teacups— so many colors! But one tea caught my eye at my local organic foods purveyer: yerba maté.

Yerba Maté	
Species	*Ilex paraguariensis*
Zone	9–10
Needs	☀☀☀ 💧💧💧
Soil pH	6.0–7.0
Size	26–60 ft. in the wild

Growing Yerba Maté

The most economical foods are those we grow ourselves, but only a reader living in an extraordinarily subtropical environment should take on the challenge of nurturing yerba maté. This plant is temperamental when grown indoors and needs high temps and much humidity. In the wild, it receives a season of heavy rainfall, which is why it flourishes below the equator in Brazil, Paraguay, and Argentina.

A yerba maté plant will need a few years before the leaves are ready to be harvested (both leaves and stems are collected). The popular tea is usually a mix of tender shoots and stems alongside older leaves. This makes for a more balanced, less "grassy" flavor.

It is possible to grow yerba maté indoors, but you will need to be consistent about its care. Make sure it gets plenty of sun and moisture. In the fall, after a few years, it can produce small white flowers. In the spring, red berries containing seeds may sprout. Given the right environment in the wild, it can grow tall very quickly, but indoors, yerba maté keeps a slower pace. You may have one for years without seeing much growth. Water frequently; the soil should be loamy and well-drained.

The Beverage

The word on this South American tea, originally an indigenous drink of the Guarani people of Paraguay, was that it would give you a lift that wouldn't include the jittery after effects of caffeine. However, yerba maté wasn't just a drink. For the past five centuries in South America, drinking it was symbolic of friendship. Yerba maté leaves were used for currency, and the Jesuits of all people were responsible for encouraging widespread industrial growth.

The traditional method of consumption is making a thick brew of ground leaves (which had been dried over a fire), in a dried gourd. You would drink the brew out of a straw made of wood or cane. The ritual involved with yerba maté could involve a few or many people who would share the calabash gourd container and *bombilla* (straw with sieve).

I have yet to share my yerba maté with another, but I have found that adding a dollop of honey to soften the earthy aroma and taste of the tea for an invigorating late afternoon beverage. I started by drinking it hot but in the summer months switched to an iced version and started experimenting with a variety of recipes.

When I brought a bag of yerba maté to a summer vacation, my brother-in-law Pat Costello, who worked in international finance, remembered his own encounter with the tea. In 1996, he was visiting Montevideo, and as he walked the streets in the afternoon hours, he saw "people gathered in knots of two or three or more, often carrying colorfully painted gourds with straws.

"My host explained that these were local people and they were drinking tea. She pointed out a vendor further down the block that was selling the liquid-filled gourds and suggested that some of the people might have packed the gourds as part of their meal to be eaten while in the city."

Pat declined trying the local street food version but later that evening "tried to find yerba maté on a menu or in the small 'city mall' but without success. It was explained that it was a local tradition—not intended for me."

But a quarter-century later, you can find yerba maté on the shelves of many mass-market grocery stores, either loose or in tea bags. And globally, it's made an impact, particularly in Syria. Nineteenth-century Syrian expats brought the drink home, and they've been drinking it ever since.

Medicinal Value

What makes yerba maté so special? It's one of the few plants that naturally produces caffeine (along with coffee, tea, kola, and cacao). A member of the holly family, this evergreen tree is found in the subtropical regions of South America. In its native habitat, it can grow ten meters or more in height.

Plus, it has a variety of bioactive components and vitamins ("A, C, E, B1, B2, Niacin, and B5"), minerals ("calcium, chromium, manganese, iron, selenium, potassium, magnesium, phosphorus, and zinc"), and polyphenols, writes pharmacy professor Irene Dini. Among the health claims by supporters of yerba maté are that drinking the tea can help aid weight loss.

In 2013, a small study in Korea led by Dr. Min-gul Kim at the Chonbuk National University Hospital was performed over twelve weeks to evaluate the effects of yerba maté "supplementation" (pills versus tea) in subjects who suffered from obesity. One group was given yerba maté; the other a placebo. At the end of the study, scientists concluded that yerba maté "was a potent anti-obesity reagent that did not produce significant adverse effects."

However, other studies, including one in the *Journal of Environmental Science and Health,* noted the presence of polycyclic aromatic hydrocarbons, or PAHs, which are known carcinogens. (You'll also find PAHs in grilled meat and tobacco smoke.) The yerba maté plant is traditionally dried over a fire, which may account for the presence of PAHs. Some companies, such as ECOTEAS, are offering an "unsmoked" version of yerba maté. I've tried both smoked and unsmoked and find them similar—but then, I like at least a teaspoon of honey in a cup of yerba maté, with a sprinkling of cinnamon as well.

At this point, yerba maté has not been studied as extensively as many other more common foods or beverages, but its growing profile in the West and parts of Europe suggest this may change. One commonality I found in a wide variety of sources—both scholarly and popular—was that chronic drinking of maté served extremely hot (149 degrees Fahrenheit) was associated with a higher risk of cancer than drinking yerba maté at cooler temperatures. Apparently, drinking super-hot yerba maté is also part of the traditional communal drinking of the tea, although the *cebador* (the host who prepares and takes the first super-hot sip) is supposed to spit it out.

Recipes

I recommend any novice yerba maté drinker try a variety with sweeteners, spices, and other additives. The earthy, natural aroma gets more complex and uniquely delicious once you start experimenting.

Western-Style Yerba Maté

Put 2 teaspoons yerba maté into your cup and lightly moisten with cold water. Pour 6 ounces hot water (not boiling) over the leaves. Let steep for no more than 5 minutes. Strain and sip. As desired, you can add sweeteners (agave, honey, maple syrup, simple syrup) or spices (cinnamon, nutmeg, coriander, or just experiment!).

Happy Happy Yerba Maté

    6 ounces cold-brewed yerba maté tea

    1 teaspoon honey

    ½ teaspoon cinnamon

    4 to 6 ounces cashew milk (or other plant, nut, or mammal milk); instructions below

Combine all ingredients and blend to a thick froth.

You can make your own cashew milk by soaking ½ cup cashew nuts in 1 cup water overnight. Drain and add 2 cups of water. Blend and store the liquid in a jar in fridge for up to 5 days.

Yerba Maté Maya: A Recipe for Love

Finally, in the course of research, I had the pleasure of speaking to people who work with yerba maté professionally. Stefan J. Schnacter is the general manager of Oregon-based ECOTEAS, which manufactures a variety of yerba maté tea products.

This recipe is designed to be used with a bombilla (straw) but can be filtered. Start by adding 2 to 3 tablespoons whole plant loose yerba maté and hot water to a 12-ounce mug, and then add your choice of additives. Stefan recommends the following:

    1 tablespoon raw organic cacao powder

    Few dashes cinnamon

    1 dash cayenne pepper

    ¼–½ cup milk of choice

Stefan also adds 1 teaspoon coconut sugar for his "sweetie's" cup. Then add not-quite-boiling water to the mix.

As you sip, do not move the straw, to avoid clogs. Sip it slowly while you welcome the new day.

Resources

Chamberlain, Michael. "Yerba Mate Plant—How to Grow It, Make It and Drink It!" *Tea How* (blog). N.d. https://teahow.com/yerba-mate-how-to-grow-make-drink/.

Dini, Irene. "An Overview of Functional Beverages." In *Functional and Medicinal Beverages*. Cambridge, MA: Academic Press, 2019. Page 24.

"History of Yerba Mate." Yerba Mate Argentina. Accessed December 7, 2020. https://yerbamateargentina.org.ar/en/yerba-mate/la-yerba-mate-y-su-historia/.

Johnstone, Gemma. "Yerba Maté Plant Profile." The Spruce. July 28, 2020. https://www.thespruce.com/yerba-mate-plant-profile-5071184.

Kim, Min-gul, Sun-young Kim, Mi-ra Oh, Han-jeoung Chae, and Soo-wan Chae. "Anti-Obesity Effects of Yerba Maté (Ilex Paraguariensis): A Randomized, Double-Blind, Placebo-Controlled Clinical Trial." *BMC Complementary and Alternative Medicine* 15, no. 338 (September 2015): n. p. https://pubmed.ncbi.nlm.nih.gov/26408319/.

Oranuba, Ebela, Hua Deng, Jiangnan Peng, Sanford M. Dawsey, and Farin Kamangar. "Polycyclic Aromatic Hydrocarbons as a Potential Source of Carcinogenicity of Mate." *Journal of Environmental Science and Health, Part C: Environmental Carcinogenesis and Ecotoxicology Reviews* 37, no. 1 (2019): 26–41. https://www.ncbi.nlm.nih.gov/pmc/articles/PMC6443446/.

Petre, Alina. "8 Health Benefits of Yerba Maté (Backed by Science)." Healthline. December 17, 2018. https://www.healthline.com/nutrition/8-benefits-of-yerba-mate#TOC_TITLE_HDR_4.

"Yerba Mate Care Guide." A Natural Farm. Last modified March 2016. https://static1.squarespace.com/static/52f70946e4b045fae91325c9/t/56eaca2c62cd946d4c7dcd54/1458227765602/Yerba+Mate+Care+Guide+3-16.pdf.

Zeratsky, Katherine. "Drinking Yerba Maté at Higher Temperatures."
    Mayo Clinic. January 15, 2019. https://www.mayoclinic.org
    /healthy-lifestyle/nutrition-and-healthy-eating/expert-answers
    /yerba-mate/faq-20058343.

Gardening
Resources

Companion Planting Guide

Group together plants that complement each other by deterring certain pests, absorbing different amounts of nutrients from the soil, shading their neighbors, and enhancing friends' flavors. This table of herbs and common garden vegetables offers suggestions for plants to pair together and plants to keep separated.

Plant	Good Pairing	Poor Pairing
Anise	Coriander	Carrot, basil, rue
Asparagus	Tomato, parsley, basil, lovage, Asteraceae spp.	
Basil	Tomato, peppers, oregano, asparagus	Rue, sage, anise
Beans	Tomato, carrot, cucumber, cabbage, corn, cauliflower, potato	Gladiola, fennel, *Allium* spp.
Bee balm	Tomato, echinacea, yarrow, catnip	
Beet	Onions, cabbage, lettuce, mint, catnip, kohlrabi, lovage	Pole bean, field mustard
Bell pepper	Tomato, eggplant, coriander, basil	Kohlrabi
Borage	Tomato, squash, strawberry	
Broccoli	Aromatics, beans, celery, potato, onion, oregano, pennyroyal, dill, sage, beet	Tomato, pole bean, strawberry, peppers
Cabbage	Mint, sage, thyme, tomato, chamomile, hyssop, pennyroyal, dill, rosemary, sage	Strawberry, grape, tomato
Carrot	Peas, lettuce, chive, radish, leek, onion, sage, rosemary, tomato	Dill, anise, chamomile

Plant	Good Pairing	Poor Pairing
Catnip	Bee balm, cucumber, chamomile, mint	
Celery	Leek, tomato, bush bean, cabbage, cauliflower, carrot, garlic	Lovage
Chamomile	Peppermint, beans, peas, onion, cabbage, cucumber, catnip, dill, tomato, pumpkin, squash	
Chervil	Radish, lettuce, broccoli	
Chive	Carrot, *Brassica* spp., tomato, parsley	Bush bean, potato, peas, soybean
Coriander/cilantro	*Plant anywhere*	Fennel
Corn	Potato, beans, peas, melon, squash, pumpkin, sunflower, soybean, cucumber	Quack grass, wheat, straw, tomato
Cucumber	Beans, cabbage, radish, sunflower, lettuce, broccoli, squash, corn, peas, leek, nasturtium, onion	Aromatic herbs, sage, potato, rue
Dill	Cabbage, lettuce, onion, cucumber	Carrot, caraway, tomato
Echinacea	Bee balm	
Eggplant	Catnip, green beans, lettuce, kale, redroot pigweed	
Fennel	*Isolate; disliked by all garden plants*	
Garlic	Tomato, rose	Beans, peas
Hyssop	*Most plants*	Radish
Kohlrabi	Green bean, onion, beet, cucumber	Tomato, strawberry, pole bean
Lavender	*Plant anywhere*	
Leek	Onion, celery, carrot, celeriac	Bush bean, soy bean, pole bean, pea

Plant	Good Pairing	Poor Pairing
Lemon balm	*All vegetables*, particularly squash, pumpkin	
Lettuce	Strawberry, cucumber, carrot, radish, dill	Pole bean, tomato
Lovage	*Most plants*, especially cucumber, beans, beet, *Brassica* spp., onion, leek, potato, tomato	Celery
Marjoram	*Plant anywhere*	
Melon	Corn, peas, morning glory	Potato, gourd
Mint	Cabbage, tomato, nettle	Parsley, rue
Nasturtium	Cabbage, cucumber, potato, pumpkin, radish	
Onion	Beets, chamomile, carrot, lettuce, strawberry, tomato, kohlrabi, summer savory	Peas, beans, sage
Oregano	*Most plants*	
Parsley	Tomato, asparagus, carrot, onion, rose	Mint, *Allium* spp.
Parsnip	Peas	
Peas	Radish, carrot, corn, cucumbers, bean, tomato, spinach, turnip, aromatic herbs	*Allium* spp., gladiola
Potato	Beans, corn, peas, cabbage, eggplant, catnip, horseradish, watermelon, nasturtium, flax	Pumpkin, raspberry, sunflower, tomato, orach, black walnut, cucumber, squash
Pumpkin	Corn, lemon balm	Potato
Radish	Peas, lettuce, nasturtium, chervil, cucumber	Hyssop
Rose	Rue, tomato, garlic, parsley, tansy	*Any plant within 1 ft. radius*
Rosemary	Rue, sage	

Plant	Good Pairing	Poor Pairing
Sage	Rosemary	Rue, onion
Spinach	Strawberry, garlic	
Squash	Nasturtium, corn, mint, catnip, radish, borage, lemon balm	Potato
Strawberry	Borage, bush bean, spinach, rue, lettuce	*Brassica* spp., garlic, kohlrabi
Tarragon	*Plant anywhere*	
Thyme	*Plant anywhere*	
Tomato	Asparagus, parsley, chive, onion, carrot, marigold, nasturtium, bee balm, nettle, garlic, celery, borage	Black walnut, dill, fennel, potato, *Brassica* spp., corn
Turnip	Peas, beans, brussels sprout, leek	Potato, tomato
Yarrow	*Plant anywhere*, especially with medicinal herbs	

For more information on companion planting, you may wish to consult the following resources:

Mayer, Dale. *The Complete Guide to Companion Planting: Everything You Need to Know to Make Your Garden Successful.* Ocala, FL: Atlantic Publishing, 2010.

Philbrick, Helen. *Companion Plants and How to Use Them.* Edinburgh, UK: Floris Books, 2016.

Riotte, Louise. *Carrots Love Tomatoes: Secrets of Companion Planting for Successful Gardening.* Pownal, VT: Storey Books, 1988.

Cooking with Herbs and Spices

Elevate your cooking with herbs and spices. Remember, a little goes a long way!

Herb	Flavor Pairings	Health Benefits
Anise	Salads, slaws, roasted vegetables	Reduces nausea, gas, and bloating. May relieve infant colic. May help menstrual pain. Loosens sputum in respiratory illnesses.
Basil	Pesto and other pasta sauces, salads	Eases stomach cramps, nausea, indigestion, and colic. Mild sedative action.
Borage	Soups	Soothes respiratory congestion. Eases sore, inflamed skin. Mild diuretic properties.
Cayenne	Adds a spicy heat to soups, sauces, and main courses	Stimulates blood flow. Relieves joint and muscle pain. Treats gas and diarrhea.
Chamomile	Desserts, teas	Used for nausea, indigestion, gas pains, bloating, and colic. Relaxes tense muscles. Eases menstrual cramps. Promotes relaxation and sleep.
Chervil	Soups, salads, and sauces	Settles and supports digestion. Mild diuretic properties. Useful in treating minor skin irritations.
Chive	Salads, potato dishes, sauces	Rich in antioxidants. May benefit insomnia. Contributes to strong bones.
Coriander/cilantro	Soups, picante sauces, salsas	Treats mild digestive disorders. Counters nervous tensions. Sweetens breath.

Herb	Flavor Pairings	Health Benefits
Dill	Cold salads and fish dishes	Treats all types of digestive disorders, including colic. Sweetens breath. Mild diuretic.
Echinacea	Teas	Supports immune function. May treat or prevent infection.
Fennel	Salads, stir-fry, vegetable dishes	Settles stomach pain, relieves bloating, and stimulates appetite. May help treat kidney stones and bladder infections. Mild expectorant. Eye wash treats conjunctivitis.
Garlic	All types of meat and vegetable dishes as well as soup stocks and bone broths	Antiseptic: aids in wound healing. Treats and may prevent infections. Benefits the heart and circulatory system.
Ginger	Chicken, pork, stir-fry, gingerbread and ginger cookies	Treats all types of digestive disorders. Stimulates circulation. Soothes colds and flu.
Hyssop	Chicken, pasta sauces, light soups	Useful in treating respiratory problems and bronchitis. Expectorant. Soothes the digestive tract.
Jasmine	Chicken dishes, fruit desserts	Relieves tension and provides mild sedation. May be helpful in depression. Soothes dry or sensitive skin.
Lavender	Chicken, fruit dishes, ice cream	Soothes and calms the nerves. Relieves indigestion, gas, and colic. May relax airways in asthma.

Herb	Flavor Pairings	Health Benefits
Lemon balm	Soups, sauces, seafood dishes	Soothes and calms the nerves. Treats mild anxiety and depression. Helps heal wounds.
Lemongrass	Marinades, stir-fries, curries, spice rubs	Treats all types of digestive disorders. Reduces fever. May reduce pain.
Lemon verbena	Beverages, any recipe asking for lemon zest	Calms digestive problems and treats stomach pain. Gently sedative.
Lovage	Soups, lovage pesto, lentils	Acts as a digestive and respiratory tonic. Has diuretic and antimicrobial actions. Boosts circulation. Helps menstrual pain.
Marigold	Soups, salads, rice dishes	Effective treatment of minor wounds, insect bites, sunburn, acne, and other skin irritations. Benefits menstrual pain and excessive bleeding.
Marjoram	Vegetables, soups, tomato dishes, sausages	Calms the digestive system. Stimulates appetite.
Nasturtium	Nasturtium pesto, salad dressings, salads	Strong antibiotic properties. Treats wounds and respiratory infections.
Oregano	Chicken, tomato sauces and dishes	Strong antiseptic properties. Stimulates bile production. Eases flatulence.
Parsley	Soups, stocks, bone broths	Highly nutritious. Strong diuretic action and may help treat cystitis. Benefits gout, rheumatism, and arthritis.
Peppermint	Desserts, teas	Treats all types of digestive disorders. May help headaches.

Herb	Flavor Pairings	Health Benefits
Purslane	Salads	Treats digestive and bladder ailments. Mild antibiotic effects.
Rosemary	Roasted red meats, potato dishes, grilled foods	Stimulates circulation. May stimulate the adrenal glands. Elevates mood and may benefit depression.
Sage	Chicken, duck, and pork	Relieves pain in sore throats. May help treat menstrual and menopausal disorders.
Spinach	Sautéed, soups, salads, spinach pesto, stuffed in chicken, ravioli	Iron-rich; supports healthy blood and iron stores.
Summer savory	Mushrooms, vegetables, quiche	Treats digestive and respiratory issues.
Tarragon	Chicken, fish, vegetables, sauces—"classic French cooking"	Stimulates digestion. Promotes sleep—mildly sedative. Induces menstruation.
Thyme	Soups, stews, tomato-based sauces	May treat infections. Soothes sore throats and hay fever. Can help expel parasites. Relieves minor skin irritations.
Winter-green	Ice cream, candies, desserts	Strong anti-inflammatory and antiseptic properties. Treats arthritis and rheumatism. Relieves flatulence.
Winter savory	Beans, meats, vegetables	Treats digestive and respiratory issues. Antibacterial properties.
Yarrow	Salad dressings, infused oils	Helps heal minor wounds. Eases menstrual pain and heavy flow. Tonic properties.

Gardening Techniques

Gardeners are creative people who are always on the lookout for the most efficient, interesting, and beautiful ways to grow their favorite plants. Whether you need to save money, reduce your workload, or keep plants indoors, the following gardening techniques are just a sampling of the many ways to grow your very own bountiful garden.

Barrel

Lidless plastic food-grade barrels or drums are set on raised supports. Before the barrel is filled with soil, slits are cut into the sides of the barrel and shaped into pockets. A PVC pipe is perforated with holes and set into the center and out of the bottom of the barrel as a delivery tool for watering, draining, fertilizing, and feeding the optional worm farm.

Strengths

Initial cost is moderate. Retains moisture, warms quickly, drains well, takes up little space, maximizes growing area, and repels burrowing rodents. Little weeding or back-bending required.

Weaknesses

Not always attractive, initially labor intensive, requires special tools to modify. Not generally suited for crops that are deep-rooted, large vining, or traditionally grown in rows, such as corn.

Hügelkultur

These permanent raised beds utilize decomposing logs and woody brush that have been stacked into a pyramidal form on top of the soil's surface or in shallow trenches and then packed and covered with eight to ten inches of soil, compost, and well-rotted manure. The rotting wood encourages soil biota while holding and releasing moisture to plants, much like a sponge. English pronunciation: "hoogle-culture."

Strengths
Vertical form warms quickly, drains well, reduces watering needs, increases overall planting surface, and reduces bending chores. In time the rotting wood breaks down into humus-rich soil.

Weaknesses
Labor-intensive construction and mulch tends to slide down sides. Requires two to three years of nitrogen supplementation, repeated soaking, and filling sunken voids with soil. Voids can also be attractive to rodents and snakes in the first few years.

Hydroponic
Hydroponics is based on a closed (greenhouse) system relying on carefully timed circulation of nutrient-enriched water flowing through a soilless growing medium in which plants grow. Aerial parts are supported above the water by rafts and, at times, vertical supports. With the addition of fish tanks to the system, hydroponics becomes aquaponics.

Strengths
Customizable to any size. Versatile, efficient, productive, and weedless. Produce stays clean.

Weaknesses

Large systems are expensive and complicated to set up and maintain; require multiple inputs of heat, light, and nutrients; and are limited to certain crop types.

Lasagna

Based on sheet composting, lasagna gardens are built up in layers, starting with paper or cardboard that is placed on top of turf-covered or tilled ground to smother weeds and feed ground worm activity. This is then covered in repeating layers of peat moss, compost, leaves, wood chips, manure, and yard waste (green, brown, green), which eventually break down into rich, humusy soil.

Strengths

Excellent natural method to enrich poor soils, utilizes organic waste, supports soil biota, and improves drainage while reducing the need for fertilizers and excessive watering.

Weaknesses

Initially labor intensive and the proper breakdown of bed materials takes months, so is not suited to "quick" gardening. Requires ready and abundant sources of clean, unsprayed, organic materials.

Ruth Stout

This "no work" garden is based on deep, permanent layers of progressively rotting straw mulch, which simultaneously builds soil, feeds plants, blocks weeds, and reduces watering. Seeds and plants are placed into the lower decomposed layers. Fresh straw is added as plants grow and kept at a depth of eight or more inches.

Strengths

No tilling, few weeds, reduced watering and fertilizing. Warms quickly in the spring and prevents winter heaving. An excellent method for rocky, sandy, or clay soils.

Weaknesses

Requires an abundance of straw each season, which can be expensive and difficult to transport, move, and store. Deep mulch may encourage burrowing rodents and provide shelter for slugs, insect pests, and diseases.

Soil Bag

This simple method utilizes one or more twenty- to forty-pound bags of commercial potting soil or topsoil simply laid out flat on turf, mulch, or wood pallets. A rectangular hole is cut into the top and drainage holes are punched through the bottom. A light dusting of fertilizer is mixed in and plants and seeds are sown.

Strengths

Super easy, weed-free, no-till garden and a great way to start an in-ground garden. Fun for kids and those without a yard.

Weaknesses

Limited to shallow-rooted crops, needs consistent watering and fertilizing, and may flood in heavy rains. Cats may find this an attractive litter box.

Straw Bale

One or more square, string-bound straw bales are placed cut side up either directly on the ground or on top of a weed barrier and soaked with water for several days or even months and treated with nitrogen to help speed the decomposition of the straw. Alternatively, bales can be overwintered in place before using. Once ready, bales are parted down the center, filled with soil and compost, and planted with seeds or starts.

Strengths
Good on poor soils, even concrete. No tilling required, few weeds, handicap accessible, versatile, easy to configure, and renter-friendly. Spent bales make excellent mulch.

Weaknesses
Straw bales can be expensive, heavy, and difficult to transport. These gardens can initially be labor intensive, require frequent watering and fertilizing, and must be replaced every one or two seasons. Nitrogen from treated bales can leach into the local environment and affect the watershed.

Square Foot
This modern take on French Intensive gardening utilizes raised beds filled with a special soilless blend enclosed in a box frame that is further divided into twelve-by-twelve-inch squares, or one square foot. Each square is planted or seeded based on the correct spacing requirements of each plant. Large crops, like tomatoes, are planted one to a square, while small crops like radishes are planted sixteen to a square.

Strengths
Proper plant spacing utilizes space, increases yields, and reduces weeds. Adding trellises increases growing capacity. Raised beds drain well, warm quickly, hold mulch, look tidy, and are easy to mow around.

Weaknesses

Initial construction is expensive, labor intensive, and often impermanent. Requires frequent watering in dry spells, and not all crops are suitable. Grids can be tedious to use and do not remove the gardener's need to learn proper plant spacing.

Vertical

Vertical gardens make use of nontraditional gardening space in two ways. The first is by training vining and climbing plants onto trellises, arbors, or fences and growing in raised beds, pots, urns, or tubs. The second is by firmly securing containers, troughs, rain gutters, or vertical garden felt pockets onto permanent frames supported by fences, walls, or other sturdy vertical structures. These gardens are typically irrigated by automatic drip or hydroponic systems. Soilless options are available.

Strengths

Attractive and weed-free indoor-outdoor garden perfect for small yards, renters, and disabled persons. Helps hide ugly structures and views and defines outdoor spaces.

Weaknesses

Construction of large systems and very sturdy structures can be initially expensive or labor intensive. Not conducive to all garden crops and requires frequent and consistent applications of moisture and fertilizer.

2022 Themed Garden Plans

Mr. MacGregor's Garden

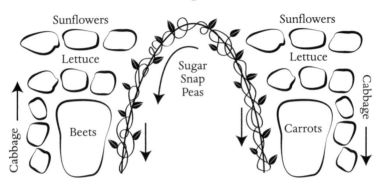

Fit for Peter Rabbit himself, this little garden is filled with classic veggies and may include a fanciful arbor for easy access to climbing vegetables such as peas, cucumbers, or beans. A great garden plan to get the kids excited about eating their veggies.

Hardy Winter Garden

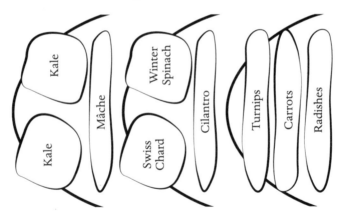

Enjoy fresh, nutritious greens all year round with this wonderful variety of cold-hardy vegetables. For added protection of your winter garden bed, use 10-ft. lengths of ½-in. PVC pipe bent over 4-ft. wide garden beds and slipped onto 12-in. rebar stakes every 3–4 in. Cover with greenhouse poly and secure to PVC pipe with easy-snap clamps.

Midnight Garden

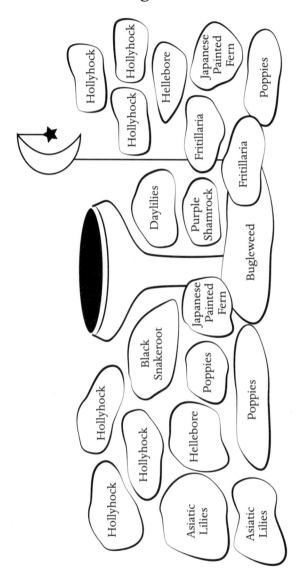

A perfect garden for those gothic at heart. Enjoy rich, dark blooms an foliage variet-ies from common cottage garden favorites. This little garden will definitely add a wee bit of magic to your garden space.

Planning Your 2022 Garden

Prepare your soil by tilling and fertilizing. Use the grid on the right, enlarging on a photocopier if needed, to sketch your growing space and identify sunny and shady areas.

Plot Shade and Sun

Watch your yard or growing space for a day, checking at regular intervals (such as once an hour), and note the areas that receive sun and shade. This will shift over the course of your growing season. Plant accordingly.

Diagram Your Space

Consider each plant's spacing needs before planting. Vining plants, such as cucumbers, will sprawl out and require trellising or a greater growing area than root crops like carrots. Be sure to avoid pairing plants that naturally compete or harm each other (see the Companion Planting Guide on page 256).

Also consider if your annual plants need to be rotated. Some herbs will reseed, some can be planted in the same place year after year, and some may need to be moved after depleting the soil of certain nutrients during the previous growing season.

Determine Your Last Spring Frost Date

Using data from the previous year, estimate the last spring frost date for your area and note what you'll need to plant before or after this date. Refer to seed packets, plant tags, and experts at your local garden center or University Extension for the ideal planting time for each plant.

My 2022 last spring frost date: _____

Growing Space Grid

☐ = _____ feet

January

Task	Plants	Dates

Notes:

_____

_____

_____

_____

_____

_____

_____

JANUARY

						1
●	3	4	5	6	7	8
◑	10	11	12	13	14	15
16	○	18	19	20	21	22
23	24	◑	26	27	28	29
30	31					

Planning Your Garden

When it is cold and dreary out, it is a good time to imagine your spring garden. Use a pencil, paper, and graph paper (or use page 273) to draw out what you would like to plant where. Think about the mature sizes of plants and place companions together.

February

Task	Plants	Dates

Notes:

_____

_____

_____

_____

_____

_____

_____

Sow Tiny Seeds

Late February is time to start sowing the slowest-growing plants indoors under a plant light. These are plants with the tiniest of seeds. Start early annuals (like pansy, petunia, and rose), vegetables (onions, leeks, and celery), and herbs (rosemary, thyme, parsley, and lavender).

FEBRUARY

		●	2	3	4	5
6	7	☾	9	10	11	12
13	14	15	○	17	18	19
20	21	22	☽	24	25	26
27	28					

March

Task	Plants	Dates

Notes:

_____

_____

_____

_____

_____

_____

_____

MARCH

				1	●	3	4	5
6	7	8	9	◐	11	12
13	14	15	16	17	○	19
20	21	22	23	24	◑	26
27	28	29	30	31

Reusing Pots

Plastic pots for planting seeds can be reused for many years—until they literally fall apart. Clean them thoroughly by soaking in 10% bleach solution for 20 minutes or running them through the dishwasher. Small seedlings are sensitive to the pathogens on used pots.

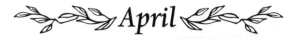

April

Task	Plants	Dates

Notes:

_____

_____

_____

_____

_____

_____

_____

Working Your Soil

Once your garden soil is workable, it is time to start planting outside. Make sure the soil is fully thawed and not muddy. Layer on an inch of compost and gently work it in before you plant. The first seeds to go in include peas, radishes, spinach, dill, and cilantro.

APRIL

					●	2
3	4	5	6	7	8	◖
10	11	12	13	14	15	○
17	18	19	20	21	22	◗
24	25	26	27	28	29	●

May

Task	Plants	Dates

Notes:

_____

_____

_____

_____

_____

_____

_____

MAY						
1	2	3	4	5	6	7
◑	9	10	11	12	13	14
15	○	17	18	19	20	21
◐	23	24	25	26	27	28
29	●	31				

Phenology

There are some great old reminders of when to plant seeds outside. Plant corn when oak leaves are as big as squirrels' ears. When dandelions bloom, plant potatoes, beets, lettuce, spinach, and carrots. When the lilacs bloom, plant beans, cucumbers, and squash.

June

Task	Plants	Dates

Notes:

_____

_____

_____

_____

_____

_____

_____

Succession Planting

Planting the same plant over and over can extend your herb and vegetable harvests. Every 3 or 4 weeks until mid-July, plant a new row of dill, cilantro, lettuce, arugula, spinach, beets, carrots, green beans, and radishes.

JUNE

			1	2	3	4
5	6	☽	8	9	10	11
12	13	○	15	16	17	18
19	◑	21	22	23	24	25
26	27	●	29	30		

July

Task	Plants	Dates

Notes:

_____

_____

_____

_____

_____

_____

_____

_____

JULY

					1	2
3	4	5	◑	7	8	9
10	11	12	○	14	15	16
17	18	19	◑	21	22	23
24	25	26	27	●	29	30
31						

July Is Time for Weeding!

While it is fun to use July to get to know the names of each weed, it is also a good time to layer on mulch to suppress their growth. Hay is a great product to use. Use either aged or heat-treated hay so you will not be adding more weed seeds to your soil.

August

Task	Plants	Dates

Notes:

_____

_____

_____

_____

_____

_____

_____

Mildew-Resistant Basil Varieties

It is a recent thing to have to plan for basil mildew, a disease that began in the US in the early 2000s and kills most varieties by August. Check varieties for resistance so your harvest will last until frost. Resistant varieties to try include 'Prospera', 'Rutgers', and 'Thunderstruck'.

AUGUST

	1	2	3	4	◐ 5	6
7	8	9	10	○	12	13
14	15	16	17	18	◑ 19	20
21	22	23	24	25	26	●
28	29	30	31			

September

Task	Plants	Dates

Notes:

_____

_____

_____

_____

_____

_____

_____

SEPTEMBER

				1	2	☽
4	5	6	7	8	9	○
11	12	13	14	15	16	☾
18	19	20	21	22	23	24
●	26	27	28	29	30	

Preserving Vegetables

Almost any vegetable can be canned, fermented, or made into a delicious pickle! September is a great time to experiment with different recipes. Use vegetables and herbs from your garden or fresh from the local farm stand.

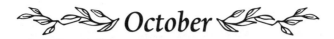

October

Task	Plants	Dates

Notes:

_____

_____

_____

_____

_____

_____

_____

Drying Herbs

Harvest your herbs before fall frost and dry them for use all winter. Dry small-leaved herbs by hanging in bunches (dill, thyme, and rosemary). Dry large-leaved herbs in an oven or dehydrator (basil, sage, and parsley). Once dry, crumble and store herbs in airtight containers.

OCTOBER

						1
◑	3	4	5	6	7	8
○	10	11	12	13	14	15
16	◐	18	19	20	21	22
23	24	●	26	27	28	29
30	31					

November

Task	Plants	Dates

Notes:

_____

_____

_____

_____

_____

_____

_____

NOVEMBER

		◑	2	3	4	5
6	7	○	9	10	11	12
13	14	15	◑	17	18	19
20	21	22	●	24	25	26
27	28	29	◑			

Planting Garlic

Tradition says to plant garlic bulbs on the shortest day of the year. In many areas the ground is frozen solid by then. In Northern areas, plant garlic a month before the ground freezes—November at the latest.

December

Task	Plants	Dates

Notes:

_____

_____

_____

_____

_____

_____

_____

Homemade Gifts

Sharing your garden produce is one of the most rewarding things for a gardener. Gifts you can make include dried herbs in pretty jars, bunches of lavender tied with a bow, herb-infused oils, and brightly colored jams and jellies. Try making simple handmade labels to decorate these.

DECEMBER

				1	2	3
4	5	6	○	8	9	10
11	12	13	14	15	◐	17
18	19	20	21	22	●	24
25	26	27	28	◑	30	31

Gardening by the Moon

It is believed that the moon's gravitational pull extends beyond Earth's oceans, affecting the moisture in the soil, seeds, and plants. Some gardeners utilize this timing to strategically plan various gardening activities.

Gardening by Moon Phase

During the waxing moon (from new moon to full moon), plant annuals, crops that need to be seeded anew each year, and those that produce their yield above the ground. During the waning moon (from full moon to new moon), plant biennials, perennials, and bulb and root plants. As a rule, these are plants that produce below the ground.

These are not hard and fast divisions. If you can't plant during the first quarter, plant during the second, and vice versa. There are many plants that seem to do equally well planted in either quarter, such as watermelon, hay, and cereals and grains.

First Quarter (Waxing): The first quarter begins with the new moon. Plant annuals that produce their yield above the ground and are generally of the leafy kind that produce their seed outside their fruit. Examples are asparagus, broccoli, brussels sprouts, cabbage, cauliflower, celery, cress, endive, kohlrabi, lettuce, parsley, and spinach. Cucumbers are an exception, as they do best in the first quarter rather than the second, even though the seeds are inside the fruit. Also in the first quarter, plant cereals and grains.

Second Quarter (Waxing): Plant annuals that produce their yield above ground and are generally the viney types that produce their seed inside the fruit. Examples include beans, eggplant, melons, peas, peppers, pumpkins, squash, and tomatoes.

Third Quarter (Waning): The third quarter begins with the full moon. Plant biennials, perennials, and bulb and root plants. Also plant trees, shrubs, berries, beets, carrots, onions, parsnips, peanuts, potatoes, radishes, rhubarb, rutabagas, strawberries, turnips, winter wheat, and grapes.

Fourth Quarter (Waning): This is the best time to cultivate, turn sod, pull weeds, and destroy pests of all kinds, especially when the moon is in the barren signs of Aries, Leo, Virgo, Gemini, Aquarius, and Sagittarius.

Gardening by Moon Sign

Some gardeners include the influence of the twelve astrological signs in their lunar gardening as well. The moon changes sign roughly every two and a half days.

Moon in Aries: Barren and dry. Used for destroying noxious growth, weeds, pests, and so on, and for cultivating.

Moon in Taurus: Productive and moist. Used for planting many crops, particularly potatoes and root crops, and when hardiness is important. Also used for lettuce, cabbage, and similar leafy vegetables.

Moon in Gemini: Barren and dry. Used for destroying noxious growths, weeds, and pests, and for cultivation.

Moon in Cancer: Very fruitful and moist. This is the most productive sign, used extensively for planting and irrigation.

Moon in Leo: Barren and dry. This is the most barren sign, used only for killing weeds and for cultivation.

Moon in Virgo: Barren and moist. Good for cultivation and destroying weeds and pests.

Moon in Libra: Semi-fruitful and moist. Used for planting many crops and producing good pulp growth and roots. A very good sign for flowers and vines. Also used for seeding hay, corn fodder, etc.

Moon in Scorpio: Very fruitful and moist. Nearly as productive as Cancer; used for the same purposes. Especially good for vine growth and sturdiness.

Moon in Sagittarius: Barren and dry. Used for planting onions, for seeding hay, and for cultivation.

Moon in Capricorn: Productive and dry. Used for planting potatoes, tubers, etc.

Moon in Aquarius: Barren and dry. Used for cultivation and destroying noxious growths, weeds, and pests.

Moon in Pisces: Very fruitful and moist. Used along with Cancer and Scorpio, and especially good for root growth.

Planting Guide for Moon Phase and Sign

The following table shows how to combine the moon's quarters and signs to choose the best planting dates for crops, flowers, and trees.

Plant	*Quarter*	*Sign*
Annuals	1st or 2nd	*See specific entry*
Apple trees	2nd or 3rd	Cancer, Pisces, Taurus
Asparagus	1st	Cancer, Scorpio, Pisces
Barley	1st or 2nd	Cancer, Pisces, Libra, Capricorn
Beans	2nd	Cancer, Pisces, Libra, Taurus
Beets	3rd	Cancer, Pisces, Libra, Capricorn
Berries	2nd	Cancer, Scorpio, Pisces
Biennials	3rd or 4th	*See specific entry*
Broccoli	1st	Cancer, Scorpio, Pisces, Libra
Brussels sprouts	1st	Cancer, Scorpio, Pisces, Libra

Plant	Quarter	Sign
Buckwheat	1st or 2nd	Capricorn
Bulbs	3rd	Cancer, Scorpio, Pisces
Bulbs for seed	2nd or 3rd	*See specific entry*
Cabbage	1st	Cancer, Scorpio, Pisces, Taurus
Cantaloupes	1st or 2nd	Cancer, Scorpio, Pisces, Taurus
Carrots	3rd	Cancer, Scorpio, Pisces, Libra
Cauliflower	1st	Cancer, Scorpio, Pisces, Libra
Celery	1st	Cancer, Scorpio, Pisces
Cereals	1st or 2nd	Cancer, Scorpio, Pisces, Libra
Chard	1st or 2nd	Cancer, Scorpio, Pisces
Chicory	2nd or 3rd	Cancer, Scorpio, Pisces
Clover	1st or 2nd	Cancer, Scorpio, Pisces
Corn	1st	Cancer, Scorpio, Pisces
Corn for fodder	1st or 2nd	Libra
Cress	1st	Cancer, Scorpio, Pisces
Cucumbers	1st	Cancer, Scorpio, Pisces
Deciduous trees	2nd or 3rd	Cancer, Scorpio, Pisces, Virgo
Eggplant	2nd	Cancer, Scorpio, Pisces, Libra
Endive	1st	Cancer, Scorpio, Pisces, Libra
Flowers	1st	Taurus, Virgo, Cancer, Scorpio, Pisces, Libra
Garlic	3rd	Libra, Taurus, Pisces
Gourds	1st or 2nd	Cancer, Scorpio, Pisces, Libra
Melons	2nd	Cancer, Scorpio, Pisces
Onion seeds	2nd	Scorpio, Cancer, Sagittarius
Onion sets	3rd or 4th	Libra, Taurus, Pisces, Cancer
Parsley	1st	Cancer, Scorpio, Pisces, Libra
Parsnips	3rd	Cancer, Scorpio, Pisces, Taurus
Peach trees	2nd or 3rd	Taurus, Libra, Virgo

Plant	Quarter	Sign
Peanuts	3rd	Cancer, Scorpio, Pisces
Pear trees	2nd or 3rd	Taurus, Libra, Virgo
Perennials	3rd	*See specific entry*
Plum trees	2nd or 3rd	Taurus, Libra, Virgo
Pole beans	1st or 2nd	Scorpio
Potatoes	3rd	Cancer, Scorpio, Taurus, Libra
Pumpkins	2nd	Cancer, Scorpio, Pisces, Libra
Quinces	1st or 2nd	Capricorn
Radishes	3rd	Libra, Taurus, Pisces, Capricorn
Rice	1st or 2nd	Scorpio
Roses	1st or 2nd	Cancer
Rutabagas	3rd	Cancer, Scorpio, Pisces, Taurus
Sage	3rd	Cancer, Scorpio, Pisces
Salsify	1st or 2nd	Cancer, Scorpio, Pisces
Spinach	1st	Cancer, Scorpio, Pisces
Squash	2nd	Cancer, Scorpio, Taurus, Libra
Strawberries	3rd	Cancer, Scorpio, Pisces
String beans	1st or 2nd	Taurus
Sunflowers	2nd, 3rd, 4th	Cancer, Libra
Tomatoes	2nd	Cancer, Scorpio, Pisces, Capricorn
Tulips	1st or 2nd	Libra, Virgo
Turnips	3rd	Cancer, Scorpio, Pisces, Taurus
Watermelon	1st or 2nd	Cancer, Scorpio, Pisces, Libra

2022 Moon Signs and Phases

Cross reference the following month-by-month tables with the planting guide for moon phase and sign to determine the best planting times for 2022. Gray rows indicate the day of a phase change. All times are in Eastern Standard and Eastern Daylight Time, so be sure to adjust for your time zone.

January 2022

Date	Sign	Phase
1 Sat 6:02 pm	Capricorn	4th
2 Sun	Capricorn	New 1:33 pm
3 Mon 5:44 pm	Aquarius	1st
4 Tue	Aquarius	1st
5 Wed 7:17 pm	Pisces	1st
6 Thu	Pisces	1st
7 Fri	Pisces	1st
8 Sat 12:26 am	Aries	1st
9 Sun	Aries	2nd 1:11 pm
10 Mon 9:47 am	Taurus	2nd
11 Tue	Taurus	2nd
12 Wed 10:08 pm	Gemini	2nd
13 Thu	Gemini	2nd
14 Fri	Gemini	2nd
15 Sat 11:11 am	Cancer	2nd
16 Sun	Cancer	2nd
17 Mon 11:03 pm	Leo	Full 6:48 pm
18 Tue	Leo	3rd
19 Wed	Leo	3rd
20 Thu 9:02 am	Virgo	3rd
21 Fri	Virgo	3rd
22 Sat 5:03 pm	Libra	3rd
23 Sun	Libra	3rd
24 Mon 10:57 pm	Scorpio	3rd
25 Tue	Scorpio	4th 8:41 am
26 Wed	Scorpio	4th
27 Thu 2:34 am	Sagittarius	4th
28 Fri	Sagittarius	4th
29 Sat 4:09 am	Capricorn	4th
30 Sun	Capricorn	4th
31 Mon 4:43 am	Aquarius	4th

February 2022

Date	Sign	Phase
1 Tue	Aquarius	New 12:46 am
2 Wed 6:00 am	Pisces	1st
3 Thu	Pisces	1st
4 Fri 9:57 am	Aries	1st
5 Sat	Aries	1st
6 Sun 5:52 pm	Taurus	1st
7 Mon	Taurus	1st
8 Tue	Taurus	2nd 8:50 am
9 Wed 5:27 am	Gemini	2nd
10 Thu	Gemini	2nd
11 Fri 6:27 pm	Cancer	2nd
12 Sat	Cancer	2nd
13 Sun	Cancer	2nd
14 Mon 6:17 am	Leo	2nd
15 Tue	Leo	2nd
16 Wed 3:42 pm	Virgo	Full 11:56 am
17 Thu	Virgo	3rd
18 Fri 10:51 pm	Libra	3rd
19 Sat	Libra	3rd
20 Sun	Libra	3rd
21 Mon 4:19 am	Scorpio	3rd
22 Tue	Scorpio	3rd
23 Wed 8:29 am	Sagittarius	4th 5:32 pm
24 Thu	Sagittarius	4th
25 Fri 11:27 am	Capricorn	4th
26 Sat	Capricorn	4th
27 Sun 1:36 pm	Aquarius	4th
28 Mon	Aquarius	4th

March 2022

Date	Sign	Phase
1 Tue 3:53 pm	Pisces	4th
2 Wed	Pisces	New 12:35 pm
3 Thu 7:52 pm	Aries	1st
4 Fri	Aries	1st
5 Sat	Aries	1st
6 Sun 3:00 am	Taurus	1st
7 Mon	Taurus	1st
8 Tue 1:40 pm	Gemini	1st
9 Wed	Gemini	1st
10 Thu	Gemini	2nd 5:45 am
11 Fri 2:24 am	Cancer	2nd
12 Sat	Cancer	2nd
13 Sun 3:32 pm	Leo	2nd
14 Mon	Leo	2nd
15 Tue	Leo	2nd
16 Wed 12:59 am	Virgo	2nd
17 Thu	Virgo	2nd
18 Fri 7:26 am	Libra	Full 3:18 am
19 Sat	Libra	3rd
20 Sun 11:45 am	Scorpio	3rd
21 Mon	Scorpio	3rd
22 Tue 2:59 pm	Sagittarius	3rd
23 Wed	Sagittarius	3rd
24 Thu 5:54 pm	Capricorn	3rd
25 Fri	Capricorn	4th 1:37 am
26 Sat 8:55 pm	Aquarius	4th
27 Sun	Aquarius	4th
28 Mon	Aquarius	4th
29 Tue 12:32 am	Pisces	4th
30 Wed	Pisces	4th
31 Thu 5:30 am	Aries	4th

April 2022

Date	Sign	Phase
1 Fri	Aries	New 2:24 am
2 Sat 12:50 pm	Taurus	1st
3 Sun	Taurus	1st
4 Mon 11:04 pm	Gemini	1st
5 Tue	Gemini	1st
6 Wed	Gemini	1st
7 Thu 11:30 am	Cancer	1st
8 Fri	Cancer	1st
9 Sat	Cancer	2nd 2:48 am
10 Sun 12:00 am	Leo	2nd
11 Mon	Leo	2nd
12 Tue 10:07 am	Virgo	2nd
13 Wed	Virgo	2nd
14 Thu 4:46 pm	Libra	2nd
15 Fri	Libra	2nd
16 Sat 8:23 pm	Scorpio	Full 2:55 pm
17 Sun	Scorpio	3rd
18 Mon 10:16 pm	Sagittarius	3rd
19 Tue	Sagittarius	3rd
20 Wed 11:52 pm	Capricorn	3rd
21 Thu	Capricorn	3rd
22 Fri	Capricorn	3rd
23 Sat 2:17 am	Aquarius	4th 7:56 am
24 Sun	Aquarius	4th
25 Mon 6:15 am	Pisces	4th
26 Tue	Pisces	4th
27 Wed 12:10 pm	Aries	4th
28 Thu	Aries	4th
29 Fri 8:19 pm	Taurus	4th
30 Sat	Taurus	New 4:28 pm

May 2022

Date	Sign	Phase
1 Sun	Taurus	1st
2 Mon 6:47 am	Gemini	1st
3 Tue	Gemini	1st
4 Wed 7:05 pm	Cancer	1st
5 Thu	Cancer	1st
6 Fri	Cancer	1st
7 Sat 7:50 am	Leo	1st
8 Sun	Leo	2nd 8:21 pm
9 Mon 6:53 pm	Virgo	2nd
10 Tue	Virgo	2nd
11 Wed	Virgo	2nd
12 Thu 2:34 am	Libra	2nd
13 Fri	Libra	2nd
14 Sat 6:34 am	Scorpio	2nd
15 Sun	Scorpio	2nd
16 Mon 7:50 am	Sagittarius	Full 12:14 am
17 Tue	Sagittarius	3rd
18 Wed 8:02 am	Capricorn	3rd
19 Thu	Capricorn	3rd
20 Fri 8:53 am	Aquarius	3rd
21 Sat	Aquarius	3rd
22 Sun 11:49 am	Pisces	4th 2:43 pm
23 Mon	Pisces	4th
24 Tue 5:39 pm	Aries	4th
25 Wed	Aries	4th
26 Thu	Aries	4th
27 Fri 2:22 am	Taurus	4th
28 Sat	Taurus	4th
29 Sun 1:23 pm	Gemini	4th
30 Mon	Gemini	New 7:30 am
31 Tue	Gemini	1st

June 2022

Date	Sign	Phase
1 Wed 1:49 am	Cancer	1st
2 Thu	Cancer	1st
3 Fri 2:38 pm	Leo	1st
4 Sat	Leo	1st
5 Sun	Leo	1st
6 Mon 2:22 am	Virgo	1st
7 Tue	Virgo	2nd 10:48 am
8 Wed 11:23 am	Libra	2nd
9 Thu	Libra	2nd
10 Fri 4:41 pm	Scorpio	2nd
11 Sat	Scorpio	2nd
12 Sun 6:31 pm	Sagittarius	2nd
13 Mon	Sagittarius	2nd
14 Tue 6:14 pm	Capricorn	Full 7:52 am
15 Wed	Capricorn	3rd
16 Thu 5:44 pm	Aquarius	3rd
17 Fri	Aquarius	3rd
18 Sat 7:01 pm	Pisces	3rd
19 Sun	Pisces	3rd
20 Mon 11:37 pm	Aries	4th 11:11 pm
21 Tue	Aries	4th
22 Wed	Aries	4th
23 Thu 7:58 am	Taurus	4th
24 Fri	Taurus	4th
25 Sat 7:13 pm	Gemini	4th
26 Sun	Gemini	4th
27 Mon	Gemini	4th
28 Tue 7:53 am	Cancer	New 10:52 pm
29 Wed	Cancer	1st
30 Thu 8:40 pm	Leo	1st

July 2022

Date	Sign	Phase
1 Fri	Leo	1st
2 Sat	Leo	1st
3 Sun 8:31 am	Virgo	1st
4 Mon	Virgo	1st
5 Tue 6:25 pm	Libra	1st
6 Wed	Libra	2nd 10:14 pm
7 Thu	Libra	2nd
8 Fri 1:15 am	Scorpio	2nd
9 Sat	Scorpio	2nd
10 Sun 4:34 am	Sagittarius	2nd
11 Mon	Sagittarius	2nd
12 Tue 5:01 am	Capricorn	2nd
13 Wed	Capricorn	Full 2:38 pm
14 Thu 4:13 am	Aquarius	3rd
15 Fri	Aquarius	3rd
16 Sat 4:18 am	Pisces	3rd
17 Sun	Pisces	3rd
18 Mon 7:17 am	Aries	3rd
19 Tue	Aries	3rd
20 Wed 2:23 pm	Taurus	4th 10:19 am
21 Thu	Taurus	4th
22 Fri	Taurus	4th
23 Sat 1:11 am	Gemini	4th
24 Sun	Gemini	4th
25 Mon 1:54 pm	Cancer	4th
26 Tue	Cancer	4th
27 Wed	Cancer	4th
28 Thu 2:36 am	Leo	New 1:55 pm
29 Fri	Leo	1st
30 Sat 2:11 pm	Virgo	1st
31 Sun	Virgo	1st

August 2022

Date	Sign	Phase
1 Mon	Virgo	1st
2 Tue 12:06 am	Libra	1st
3 Wed	Libra	1st
4 Thu 7:47 am	Scorpio	1st
5 Fri	Scorpio	2nd 7:07 am
6 Sat 12:39 pm	Sagittarius	2nd
7 Sun	Sagittarius	2nd
8 Mon 2:39 pm	Capricorn	2nd
9 Tue	Capricorn	2nd
10 Wed 2:45 pm	Aquarius	2nd
11 Thu	Aquarius	Full 9:36 pm
12 Fri 2:44 pm	Pisces	3rd
13 Sat	Pisces	3rd
14 Sun 4:43 pm	Aries	3rd
15 Mon	Aries	3rd
16 Tue 10:22 pm	Taurus	3rd
17 Wed	Taurus	3rd
18 Thu	Taurus	3rd
19 Fri 8:06 am	Gemini	4th 12:36 am
20 Sat	Gemini	4th
21 Sun 8:29 pm	Cancer	4th
22 Mon	Cancer	4th
23 Tue	Cancer	4th
24 Wed 9:09 am	Leo	4th
25 Thu	Leo	4th
26 Fri 8:25 pm	Virgo	4th
27 Sat	Virgo	New 4:17 am
28 Sun	Virgo	1st
29 Mon 5:45 am	Libra	1st
30 Tue	Libra	1st
31 Wed 1:11 pm	Scorpio ·	1st

September 2022

Date	Sign	Phase
1 Thu	Scorpio	1st
2 Fri 6:39 pm	Sagittarius	1st
3 Sat	Sagittarius	2nd 2:08 pm
4 Sun 10:03 pm	Capricorn	2nd
5 Mon	Capricorn	2nd
6 Tue 11:41 pm	Aquarius	2nd
7 Wed	Aquarius	2nd
8 Thu	Aquarius	2nd
9 Fri 12:42 am	Pisces	2nd
10 Sat	Pisces	Full 5:59 am
11 Sun 2:47 am	Aries	3rd
12 Mon	Aries	3rd
13 Tue 7:39 am	Taurus	3rd
14 Wed	Taurus	3rd
15 Thu 4:16 pm	Gemini	3rd
16 Fri	Gemini	3rd
17 Sat	Gemini	4th 5:52 pm
18 Sun 3:59 am	Cancer	4th
19 Mon	Cancer	4th
20 Tue 4:38 pm	Leo	4th
21 Wed	Leo	4th
22 Thu	Leo	4th
23 Fri 3:53 am	Virgo	4th
24 Sat	Virgo	4th
25 Sun 12:43 pm	Libra	New 5:55 pm
26 Mon	Libra	1st
27 Tue 7:15 pm	Scorpio	1st
28 Wed	Scorpio	1st
29 Thu	Scorpio	1st
30 Fri 12:03 am	Sagittarius	1st

October 2022

Date	Sign	Phase
1 Sat	Sagittarius	1st
2 Sun 3:38 am	Capricorn	2nd 8:14 pm
3 Mon	Capricorn	2nd
4 Tue 6:20 am	Aquarius	2nd
5 Wed	Aquarius	2nd
6 Thu 8:47 am	Pisces	2nd
7 Fri	Pisces	2nd
8 Sat 11:57 am	Aries	2nd
9 Sun	Aries	Full 4:55 pm
10 Mon 5:04 pm	Taurus	3rd
11 Tue	Taurus	3rd
12 Wed	Taurus	3rd
13 Thu 1:08 am	Gemini	3rd
14 Fri	Gemini	3rd
15 Sat 12:11 pm	Cancer	3rd
16 Sun	Cancer	3rd
17 Mon	Cancer	4th 1:15 pm
18 Tue 12:45 am	Leo	4th
19 Wed	Leo	4th
20 Thu 12:25 pm	Virgo	4th
21 Fri	Virgo	4th
22 Sat 9:24 pm	Libra	4th
23 Sun	Libra	4th
24 Mon	Libra	4th
25 Tue 3:18 am	Scorpio	New 6:49 am
26 Wed	Scorpio	1st
27 Thu 6:55 am	Sagittarius	1st
28 Fri	Sagittarius	1st
29 Sat 9:21 am	Capricorn	1st
30 Sun	Capricorn	1st
31 Mon 11:43 am	Aquarius	1st

November 2022

Date	Sign	Phase
1 Tue	Aquarius	2nd 2:37 am
2 Wed 2:46 pm	Pisces	2nd
3 Thu	Pisces	2nd
4 Fri 7:07 pm	Aries	2nd
5 Sat	Aries	2nd
6 Sun	Aries	2nd
7 Mon 12:15 am	Taurus	2nd
8 Tue	Taurus	Full 6:02 am
9 Wed 8:37 am	Gemini	3rd
10 Thu	Gemini	3rd
11 Fri 7:22 pm	Cancer	3rd
12 Sat	Cancer	3rd
13 Sun	Cancer	3rd
14 Mon 7:48 am	Leo	3rd
15 Tue	Leo	3rd
16 Wed 8:04 pm	Virgo	4th 8:27 am
17 Thu	Virgo	4th
18 Fri	Virgo	4th
19 Sat 5:58 am	Libra	4th
20 Sun	Libra	4th
21 Mon 12:16 pm	Scorpio	4th
22 Tue	Scorpio	4th
23 Wed 3:16 pm	Sagittarius	New 5:57 pm
24 Thu	Sagittarius	1st
25 Fri 4:18 pm	Capricorn	1st
26 Sat	Capricorn	1st
27 Sun 5:07 pm	Aquarius	1st
28 Mon	Aquarius	1st
29 Tue 7:15 pm	Pisces	1st
30 Wed	Pisces	2nd 9:37 am

December 2022

Date	Sign	Phase
1 Thu 11:41 pm	Aries	2nd
2 Fri	Aries	2nd
3 Sat	Aries	2nd
4 Sun 6:38 am	Taurus	2nd
5 Mon	Taurus	2nd
6 Tue 3:49 pm	Gemini	2nd
7 Wed	Gemini	Full 11:08 pm
8 Thu	Gemini	3rd
9 Fri 2:49 am	Cancer	3rd
10 Sat	Cancer	3rd
11 Sun 3:09 pm	Leo	3rd
12 Mon	Leo	3rd
13 Tue	Leo	3rd
14 Wed 3:45 am	Virgo	3rd
15 Thu	Virgo	3rd
16 Fri 2:49 pm	Libra	4th 3:56 am
17 Sat	Libra	4th
18 Sun 10:31 pm	Scorpio	4th
19 Mon	Scorpio	4th
20 Tue	Scorpio	4th
21 Wed 2:12 am	Sagittarius	4th
22 Thu	Sagittarius	4th
23 Fri 2:49 am	Capricorn	New 5:17 am
24 Sat	Capricorn	1st
25 Sun 2:14 am	Aquarius	1st
26 Mon	Aquarius	1st
27 Tue 2:34 am	Pisces	1st
28 Wed	Pisces	1st
29 Thu 5:36 am	Aries	2nd 8:21 pm
30 Fri	Aries	2nd
31 Sat 12:08 pm	Taurus	2nd

Contributors

Anne Sala is a freelance writer located in Minnesota. Since the pandemic started, she has been helping her two children with their remote learning situation, becoming reacquainted with her backyard garden, and redefining what recipes qualify as "weeknight cooking."

Annie Burdick is a writer and editor living in Portland, Oregon. She has written for numerous websites, magazines, and anthologies on wildly varied topics. She is also the author of two nonfiction books, *Unconscious Bias* and *Bring the Wild Into Your Garden*, both published in 2021 by an imprint of Hachette UK. She spends most of her spare time reading, playing with her rescue dogs, and having adventures around the Pacific Northwest. Find her at annieburdickfreelance.com.

Autumn Damiana is an author, artist, crafter, amateur photographer, and regular contributor to Llewellyn's annuals. Along with writing and making art, Autumn has a degree in early childhood education. She lives with her husband and doggy familiar in the beautiful San Francisco Bay Area. Visit her online at www.autumndamiana.com.

Charlie Rainbow Wolf is happiest when she is creating something, especially if it's made from items that others have discarded. A recorded singer-songwriter and published author, she champions holistic living and lives in the Midwest with her husband and special-needs Great Danes. Astrology reports, smudge pots, smudge blends, and more are available through her website at charlierainbow.com.

Corina Sahlin has homesteaded on five acres in the Pacific Northwest for eighteen years. She has raised goats, ducks, chickens, and pigs; grows and preserves tons of organic food every year; makes cheese, soap, body-care products; and spins yarn. She teaches homesteading skills in person and online. Visit www.marblemounthomestead.com or www.corinasahlin.com.

Dawn Ritchie is an author, journalist, multimedia content provider, and TV writer/producer. Her work has appeared on all major networks, in over twenty magazines, and in national newspapers. A contributor to the 2019 and 2020 editions of *Llewellyn's Herbal Almanac*, Dawn is also an avid organic gardener, forager, cook, beekeeper, and the author of *The Emotional House* (New Harbinger Publications).

Diana Rajchel splits her time between San Francisco, California, where she co-owns Golden Apple Metaphysical, and southwestern Michigan, where she runs Earth and Sun spiritual coaching with her partner. Diana has twenty-five years' experience as a professional tarot reader and Western herbalist and has twenty-nine years' experience as a professional writer.

Elizabeth Barrette lives in central Illinois and enjoys magical crafts, historic religions, and gardening for wildlife. She has written columns on Pagan practice, speculative fiction, gender studies, and social and environmental issues. Her book *Composing Magic* explains how to combine writing and spirituality. Visit her blog at ysabetwordsmith.dreamwidth.org.

American herbalist **Holly Bellebuono** teaches internationally, has published seven books about herbal medicine and women healers, and directs a school and certification program for herbalists. Holly is the Executive Director of ACE MV, a nonprofit educational organization supporting lifelong learning, and has directed environmental and social nonprofits in North Carolina and Massachusetts.

James Kambos attributes his love of herbs and plants to the time he spent as a boy on his grandparents' farm. When not tending his garden, he can be found painting and writing from his home in the beautiful hill country of Southern Ohio.

JD Hortwort resides in North Carolina. She is an avid student of herbology and gardening. She has written a weekly garden column since 1991. She is an award-winning author, journalist, and magazine editor and a frequent contributor to the Llewellyn annuals. Her new book, *A Witch's Guide to Wildcraft*, was published by Llewellyn Publications in 2021. When not at the keyboard, she spends time in her own landscape, taking trips with friends, and with her nose buried in a book.

Jill Henderson is a backwoods herbalist, author, artist, and world traveler with a penchant for wild edible and medicinal plants, culinary herbs, and nature ecology. She is a longtime contributor to *Llewellyn's Herbal Almanac* and *Acres USA* magazine and is the author of *The Healing Power of Kitchen Herbs*, *A Journey of Seasons*, and *The Garden Seed Saving Guide*. Visit Jill's blog at www.ShowMeOz.wordpress.com.

Jordan Charbonneau is a homesteader, hiker, animal lover, and forager. She grew up in New Hampshire kayaking, hiking, and camping with her family. As an adult, she attended Sterling College (Vermont), where she double majored in ecology and environmental humanities. Today, Jordan lives in a little off-grid cabin in the hills of West Virginia with her husband, Scott. Together they grow organic vegetables and care for tons of animals.

Kathy Martin is a Master Gardener and longtime author of the blog *Skippy's Vegetable Garden*, a journal of her vegetable gardens. The blog has won awards including *Horticulture Magazine*'s Best Gardening Blog. She volunteers at gardens including the Massachusetts Horticultural Society's Gardens at Elm Bank. Kathy lives near Boston with her family, dogs, chickens, and bees.

Kathy Vilim is a Midwestern girl transplanted to Southern California who writes about the importance of creating outdoor living space using native plants and attracting pollinators. Kathy is a naturalist and photojournalist and finds herself in demand as a garden design consultant. Visit canativegardener .blogspot.com.

Linda Raedisch is a papercrafter, soapmaker, and tea enthusiast and has been writing books and articles for Llewellyn since 2011. Her most recent book is *The Lore of Old Elfland: Secrets from the Bronze Age to Middle Earth*. See her paper creations and other oddities on her Instagram page at @lindaraedisch.

Lupa is a naturalist Pagan author and artist in the Pacific Northwest. She is the author of several books on nature-based Paganism, including *Nature Spirituality From the Ground Up: Connect With Totems in Your Ecosystem* and *The Tarot of Bones* deck and book. More about Lupa and her works may be found at http://www.thegreenwolf.com

Marilyn I. Bellemore was a teacher of Colonial education at Historic New England before moving from her native Rhode Island to Vermont. She currently lives in the Green Mountains, where she makes jellies, jams, and bath and beauty products using the herbs and fruits on her hobby farm. Marilyn is the author of two traditionally published nonfiction books. She has recently written articles for *The Essential Herbal* and *Reminisce* magazines.

Melissa Tipton is a Structural Integrator, Reiki Master, and founder of Jungian Magic, which uses potent psychological insights to radically increase the efficacy of your magic. You can find more inner-journey techniques and Jungian Magic courses to improve your magic and your life at www.realmagic.school.

Mireille Blacke, MA, LADC, RD, CD-N, is a registered dietitian, licensed alcohol and drug counselor, and professor at the University of Saint Joseph in West Hartford, Connecticut. Mireille worked in rock radio for two decades before shifting her career to psychology, nutrition, and addiction counseling. She spends considerable time renovating her Victorian home, pining for New Orleans, and entertaining her beloved Bengal cats.

Monica Crosson is the author of *Wild Magical Soul, The Magickal Family,* and *Summer Sage*. She is a Master Gardener who lives in the beautiful Pacific Northwest, happily digging in the dirt and tending her raspberries with her family and their small menagerie of farm animals. Monica is a regular contributor to Llewellyn's annuals as well as *Enchanted Living Magazine* and *Witchology Magazine*.

Rachael Witt is a community herbalist, gardener, and ancestral skills teacher in the Pacific Northwest. She is the founder of Wildness Within, an herbal business that offers plant-based classes and mentorships, hand-made products, and herbal consultations. Her teachings encourage hands-on earth connections by gardening, medicine-making, and wild-tending. Learn more at www.WildnessWithinLiving.com or on Instagram at @wildnesswithinliving.

Sally Cragin is an award-winning journalist (*Boston Phoenix, Boston Globe*) and the author of *The Astrological Elements* and *Astrology on the Cusp* (Llewellyn Publications). Both books have been translated and sold in many countries including India, Russia, Canada, British Virgin Islands, the Czech Republic, and Estonia. Call 978-320-1335 or email sallycragin@verizon.net for information on consultations or group presentations.

Susan Pesznecker is a mother, writer, nurse, and college English professor living in the beautiful Pacific Northwest with her poodles. An amateur herbalist, Sue loves reading, writing, cooking, travel, and anything having to do with the outdoors. Previous works include *Crafting Magick with Pen and Ink, The Magickal Retreat*, and *Yule: Recipes & Lore for the Winter Solstice*. She's a regular contributor to the Llewellyn annuals. Follow her on Instagram at @SusanPesznecker.

Suzanne Ress runs a small farm in the Alpine foothills of Italy, where she lives with her husband. She has been a practicing Pagan for as long as she can remember and was recently featured in the exhibit "Worldwide Witches" at the Hexenmuseum of Switzerland. She is the author of *The Trial of Goody Gilbert*.

Gardening Resources

Cooking with Herbs and Spices compiled by **Susan Pesznecker**
Gardening Techniques written by **Jill Henderson**
2022 Themed Garden Plans designed by **Monica Crosson**
2022 Gardening Log tips written by **Kathy Martin**